Mother Mary Comes to Me

Words of Wisdom from Medjugorje

By Dennis Muth

Nihil obstat: Very Reverend Gary Secor, Vicar General
Approbatio: ✠Most Reverend Clarence Silva, Bishop of Honolulu
November 25, 2014

TABLE OF CONTENTS

"Dear children! Today I am calling on you to decide whether or not you wish to live the messages which I am giving you. I wish you to be active in living and spreading the messages. Especially, dear children, I wish that you all be the reflection of Jesus, which will enlighten this unfaithful world walking in darkness. I wish all of you to be the light for everyone and that you give witness in the light. Dear children, you are not called to the darkness, but you are called to the light. Therefore, live the light with your own life. Thank you for having responded to my call."

Mary's Medjugorje Message, June 5, 1986

"For Camille and Andrew, who continue to inspire me to be the best father I can be."

INTRODUCTION

My kids had known for several weeks this day would come. We were going to church, but for a reason other than for Mass. I wanted to get there early enough so we could get a good seat. Camille, in every way a seventeen-year-old, was holed up in the bathroom doing things that seventeen-year-olds do before going out. With the fairest of fair skin, freckles, and hair auburn like the setting sun, she is definitely an island girl...the island of Ireland, that is. She can be a bit stubborn at times, and yet so loving when the mood strikes. So much like her mother, I thought.

I knew we were running late and was becoming agitated while she fiddled with her hair and makeup. My sixteen-year-old son, Andrew, more like his dad than his mother in temperament, couldn't help but see my anxiousness as I paced around the house. With his laptop glued to his thighs, he sat in his favorite chair and told me we had plenty of time. My son thought the drive would take only thirty minutes, but I knew it would be at least forty. Of course, this being more than a regular Mass, I anticipated a big crowd—hence my desire to leave early. But my laid-back son assured me we had plenty of time and to stop stressing.

We finally got in the car. Hedy, my wife, wished us well, and off we went to Star of the Sea Church in Honolulu. I glanced anxiously at the clock as we pulled out of the driveway, and I was sure we would be late. If there was one thing I hated, it was being late for anything, especially church.

The drive to Honolulu from our home in Kailua was a quiet one. I played a Beatles CD to soothe my inner angst. I was filled with anxiety, and the kids sensed their dad was stressing. We were silent the entire way. *Think where you are going*, I said to myself...church, prayer, peace...I tried to fill my mind with those thoughts to calm myself down. It began to work.

We pulled up to the church parking lot only to find that it was completely full. Peace went out the window. Fortunately, they were allowing cars to park in the long driveway adjacent to the church, so we parked and got out. We entered the church, and it was standing room only. I couldn't help but look at my son with a glare of "I told you so." *Okay, snap out of it, Dennis. Enough guilt; just try and find seats for yourselves.* No luck...we had to stand. Off to the side of a pew toward the back, we were between the aisle and the outside of the church. It was okay because it was fairly cool as the trade winds came inside. I told myself I was in church now...*we're here, we made it*...no need to be grumpy with the kids. Peace, peace, peace...oh how I needed that!

Mass had barely begun, so we weren't that late. We just needed to accept that we wouldn't be sitting down for a while. We were not going to be here just for the Mass, though. There was another reason the church was overflowing with throngs of people: Ivan Dragicevic, one of the few people on earth who proclaim to see the Blessed Virgin Mary on a daily basis, would be speaking.

I had seen Ivan thirteen years earlier at our church, when he spoke in Kailua during a visit to Hawaii. I had also seen him some seven to eight years prior to that in Los Angeles and in his hometown of Medjugorje, near the border between Croatia and Bosnia-Herzegovina. This time he was en route to Australia, and Oahu was a stopover visit for him. He was here to share the message of peace, prayer, and conversion he had received from Mary, the Mother of God, to the world.

Before Ivan spoke to us, he received an apparition of the Virgin Mary inside the church, while in front of the congregation. This happened to him every day, wherever he was in the world, at 6:40 p.m. local time. From where we were standing, we saw Ivan walk up to the sanctuary in front of the altar. He knelt down with his arms stretched out slightly in front of him and his palms up, as if in a state of submission. His hair was much thinner than I remembered, and he was a bit heavier now. I had to remind myself that the years had been no kinder to me.

When the apparition began, silence filled the church. All eyes from the pews gazed upon him and the empty space in front of him where heaven stood. Occasionally, Ivan would nod his head slightly, as if conversing with Our Lady and affirming what she was saying to him. After several minutes, it was over. Memories came flooding back from when I had first seen him in what was then Yugoslavia.

So much time had come and gone since then. That was more than twenty years ago. I'm in my mid-forties now, writing about something quite personal that happened to me when I was twenty-four years old. I can't deny that what happened to me then still affects me to this day.

Like most anyone, my faith has transformed and morphed over the years. Oh yes, to say I have had my doubts would make me quite normal. I am average in every way, and still doubt on occasion. Yet there is always something I understand, see, or feel that brings me back to that place, a spiritual place that doesn't really need to exist other than in my soul. That place is Medjugorje. It's a place I didn't plan on going to, but went anyway. It's a far journey from where I grew up in Redondo Beach, California.

Chapter 1

THIS BOY

John, Paul, George, and Ringo were in the Bahamas filming *HELP!* when I was born. I was five years old when the Beatles broke up. I remember our small home at the time. My parents had their own bedroom. I shared a room with my sister, Julie. My two brothers, Dave and Dan, who were thirteen and twelve years old, shared another room. With two high-energy boys being just a year apart, you can imagine the mayhem they got into. One of my earliest childhood memories was sitting on one of the beds in their room one day. I remember that day because it was filled with drama and chaos, and someone was going to get it.

This time, Dave had said something to upset Mom. Fuming, Dad bolted into the room with his belt in hand, ready to chastise. After a few short sentences of what not to say to Mom, Dad unleashed the belt on Dave's behind. I remember his deafening screams and pleas for it to stop. From my young perspective,

I thought my brother was going to die that day. This was before Child Protective Services, so my brother had no recourse. I remember then that I was grateful to God for making me the youngest child. I owe my brothers and sister a lot, but nothing can compare to the influence they each had on me to do the right thing...or else. Despite this memory, Dad was hardly an abusive father. I rarely saw him with the belt afterward, and the tone of his voice was generally enough to keep us kids in line.

It may have been that same day as the beating, the following week, or month, but on the wall of my brothers' room was a poster of Abbey Road, the iconic photo of John, Ringo, Paul, and George walking over the now-famous crosswalk in unison near the Abbey Road studios. My brothers had the record, and I remember it being played often. The first song on side two is *You Never Give Me Your Money*. Looking back, I don't remember much about the lyrics. In fact, I'm not one to listen to lyrics of any song as much as I do the music and instrumentation.

But I do remember a lyric in that particular song which repeats at the end: *"One, two, three, four, five, six, seven—all good children go to heaven."* Why that memory has stuck with me all these decades, I can't explain. I was an impressionable kid, but it was not such a bad thing to remember.

Years of catechism and going to Sunday Mass could have been summed up in that one line. In fact, as a kid, I had forgotten that it was a Beatle lyric, but it was the lyric I retained nonetheless: "One, two, three, four, five, six, seven—all good children go to heaven." Can't our faith really be summed up in those six words: "All good children go to heaven"? As a kid, that's all I really needed to hear and know. Couple that with seeing my brother's bottom catching Dad's belt. When I was five years old, I made the decision to try to be a good kid.

For a boy, sharing a room with his sister can only be "cute" for so long. When I was seven, we moved a couple of miles away to a larger home. I was an average kid who grew up in a Southern California beach community. I pondered the existence of God, the afterlife, the Catholic Church in which I grew up, the story of Jesus, and so on. I wasn't the most straight-laced kid on the block, but I wasn't the most hell-bent, either. Religion wasn't always on my mind, yet going through twelve years of Catholic school and hanging out with friends who were predominantly Catholic, it wasn't far away either. Heaven, hell, good, and evil were always around.

Wearing my white, short-sleeved dress shirt and salt-and-pepper pants, I attended Saint Lawrence Martyr School through the eighth grade. I had a deep affection for our local church because it had brought me together with so many of my friends. Almost everyone on our block, which was within walking distance of the church, was Catholic and had big families. I think I was in fifth grade before I realized there were other Christian denominations outside of Catholicism. I went to Mass on Sunday and did my best to "lead a good life," but Catholicism was not something I was willing to die for.

I realize now how uneducated I was in matters of the Catholic faith and building a personal relationship with Christ. Having been born in 1965, I guess you could say I was a victim of the chaos as each modern church tried its best to interpret all the recent Vatican II changes, for better or for worse. Turmoil was inevitable with such long-standing traditions going by the wayside. I'm sure many were happy to see the changes come about. As could be expected, those more rooted in tradition and orthodoxy were not too excited to implement those changes.

I do remember my first Communion and first confession, lining up at the Communion rail and going into that confessional box: so dark, musty, and foreboding. Even though I knew who the priest was through the screen, the whole atmosphere changed, as if I didn't know him at all. Could he recognize my voice, I wondered? Were my sins better or worse than anyone else's? Shortly thereafter, they remodeled the confessional to accommodate "face-to- face" confessions with the priest, which I actually preferred over a totally dark environment with a shadowy silhouette peering through a screen. My inner fears began to fade once the "face-to-face" came along, and it became less intimidating and easier to confess to the priest.

Another change was abandoning the communion rail, and everyone proceeded in a line up to the front of church to receive the Eucharist in the hand. Shortly thereafter, drinking from the cup became customary. Then holding hands with those standing beside you during the Our Father. I still recall some older women refusing to hold my hand.

The 5 p.m. Mass on Sunday became interesting as they formed a choir and a band played contemporary songs. This was the age of *Godspell* and *Jesus Christ Superstar*. Blending in some upbeat rhythms seemed to follow suit with the resurgence of Christianity in pop culture at the time—especially with the younger generation.

At the time, my two older brothers and sister were teenagers. Our church at Saint Lawrence welcomed a new associate pastor, Father Doug Ferraro. He was fresh out of the seminary. He was a dark, handsome Italian and had an infectious personality and really connected with the youth of the parish. He and my parents hit it off, and in time, they were successful in establishing a youth group and teen center together. The head pastor of the church was quite old and did not associate much with us younger kids.

Father Ferraro, always finding time to join us in a game of kickball during recess, was refreshing to have around, and he gave me a very positive impression of what the priestly vocation was all about. He seemed to enjoy his calling.

Most of the teachers at the school were lay people, but about a quarter of them were nuns. They were from the Sisters of Saint Joseph of Carondelet religious order. They wore a veil and a cross necklace with stockings, long skirts and collared blouses. There were several "old school" nuns from that order—retired and quite elderly, but mobile—who lived in the convent next to the church. They wore the complete black-and-white habit, covering everything except their faces, and I wondered how they managed in the hot summer days when they were outside. I could see why the younger nuns who taught at the school had decided to be a bit less formal with the veil. Though I must say, dressed in their full habits, those older nuns seemed to exude so much holiness.

The nuns who taught at the school each had different reputations, as I'm sure they do at any Catholic school then and now. Some I absolutely feared. They weren't friendly, and detention was right around the corner if we did something over the line. Being boys, we crossed that line on frequent occasion. We never meant to hurt anyone, and thankfully, nobody ever had to go the emergency room—at least, none that I recall. Shooting spit-wads through a hollowed-out Bic pen was fun for a while, but an exciting level of danger emerged when we discovered how fast a paper clip could fly through the air from stretching it back on a rubber band between two fingers. Of course Sister "Saint" Bernard, as we called her, reminded us that an eye could have been poked out in the process. I felt obligated to let her know we weren't aiming for any kids' eyes—just their heads.

There were nuns whom my schoolmates and I actually felt were quite cool. They could relate to us and were kind and respectful. Contrary to public opinion, I was never slapped on the hands with a ruler, nor did I ever see any classmate of mine receive such physical punishment. However, when any Catholic from the Baby Boomer generation recalls their elementary school days, they are quick to remember this form of retribution. No one ever thinks that maybe such kids actually deserved it.

Mom and Dad had grown up in Chicago with neither of their parents having much money. After marrying at age twenty and having three kids, like so many looking for a warmer life in the winter, Mom and Dad took the train to sunny California before I was born. Dad secured a job, and in time was able to buy a small home in Hermosa Beach for $11,000. Through diligent saving and a tireless work ethic, my parents worked their way into a comfortable middle class lifestyle. While Dad could be a bit rigid and quick to say no to my childish whims, Mom was a bit more nurturing. When I began elementary school, she went back to work, and no matter how tired she may have been from her day, she would come home and prepare dinner. What Dad lacked in outward signs of emotion, Mom more than made up for it. When she was in a good mood, everyone around her was having a good time. She was always there to give a hug or offer an encouraging word.

It took a lot for Dad to lose his cool. He will be forever known for his dry wit and incredible moral character. I never heard him utter a swear word. Not such a big deal perhaps, but it had a very positive effect on me. As a kid, swearing could enhance your "coolness" around other foul-mouthed friends. It was easy to swear, but I thought that those who swore were not bright enough to think of any intelligent adjectives when they spoke. So with that, I tried—and still try—to not swear. Such was an example of how Dad taught me more by his example than by his words.

After Saint Lawrence, I attended a Catholic high school, but not by choice. My older brothers and sister had attended the public high school close to home. After eighth grade, many of my friends from Saint Lawrence were transferring to that school as well. Since such things are important to a kid that age, I rebelled against wanting to go to the Catholic school. I felt I had put in my time. My parents based much of their decision on the same public high school my siblings had attended as they were able to skip class, forego homework and party while still bringing home A's. My sister enjoyed her high school years a bit too much, so when I had just graduated eighth grade, Mom and Dad wanted to place me in an environment that was much more disciplined. Even after purposely flunking the entrance exam, they were on to me, and the Catholic school took me in anyhow. I despised Mom and Dad a long time after that. I considered bringing a joint to school so I could get kicked out, but after seeing the emotional anguish my parents went through with my sister, I just couldn't bear to bring them to that place again. Outside of academics and showing up to class, I refused to involve myself in the school and avoided the football games and trying out for any sports. However, I did take pleasure by involving myself in the numerous lunchtime food fights.

My sophomore year, on the evening of December 8, the feast day of Mary's Immaculate Conception, I remember watching TV with Mom and Dad. The show was interrupted by a news flash: John Lennon had been shot. I was not a huge Beatles fan at that time, but I had come to like a couple of John's songs that had been playing on the radio from his solo effort, *Double Fantasy*, which was really a comeback for him after having taken time off to raise his son, Sean. I, like the rest of the world, sat there stunned. A Beatle was dead at the age of forty. His killer, Mark David Chapman, had flown from Oahu, Hawaii, to carry out the premeditated crime. Fired from a hospital in Kailua, Chapman, a former maintenance worker, had slipped back into a dangerous mental state, flown to New York, and fixated on murdering Lennon outside his home. The world mourned for days.

The irony was not only that John Lennon strongly advocated for peace, but in the five years before his death, he had cleaned up his lifestyle of drugs, drinking, and partying to become the model husband and devoted father he never was to his first wife Cynthia and their son, Julian. Even Yoko Ono admits that when she became pregnant with Sean at the age of forty-two, after having had several miscarriages, she had contemplated abortion, but it was John who adamantly said, "No, we're going to have this baby."

The miracle of Sean in John's life was transformational and seemed to bring out the good in John. He spent those five formative years with Sean and Yoko doing nothing other than spending time together, until the music welled up enough in him to start writing again for the best-selling album, which would become *Double Fantasy*. Things could not have been going any better for John Lennon in 1980. It was a tragic end, but thankfully his music and voice will endure.

During my college years, I played in several bands as a drummer. A couple of bands were actually quite good, with creative guitarists and excellent front men as singer/songwriters. We played in some of the most popular clubs at that time in and around L.A. and Hollywood. We thought we had the potential to "make it." Unfortunately, there were about eight thousand other L.A. bands with the same idea. At times there were scouts from the record industry in the audience. We had the talent, the hooks, the songwriting, and the energetic shows. But that wasn't enough in the mid-'80s. Looking back, I now know what it was that our bands lacked: the "look." Notwithstanding the nicest of mullets, we lacked the big, long, curly, frazzled hair that was to be so characteristic of that decade. Hindsight is so 20/20.

During my initial years of college, I was in a band that played at numerous high school dances and private house parties. Private, because the parents were usually away for the weekend and didn't have a clue their teenage child was hosting a party for four surrounding high schools and their respective student bodies. A handful of girls who were mutual friends liked to come out and see us play. One of them always stood out to me. Her name was Hedy.

Like most of our following, they were into simple partying, drinking, and dancing. Hedy stood out because, unlike most of the girls, she was usually sober and the designated driver. She was always composed and didn't need a drink to have fun. That attracted me to her, but the fact that she was Chilean was a huge bonus. Her tanned complexion, thick brown hair, large brown eyes, and petite figure were something to behold. She stood out among the many beach-blonde girls of that community.

We had a mutual friend in Mike, the guitarist in my band. It really wasn't until Hedy was a freshman and I a sophomore at the community college that we had our first date, around 1985. Her parents were very protective of their only daughter and were smart for not trusting young American boys with her. For this reason, Hedy was quite shy and reserved in social settings and rarely dated in high school.

A year before, we had one date where she hardly said a word nor took a bite of her dinner —she was so nervous. I later found out she had a terrible crush on me. I took her shyness as a signal that I just wasn't her type and I should give up. When I dropped her off at her parents' home, I leaned over to give her a kiss in the front seat of my car. She gave me her cheek and was out the car door before I could un-pucker. That solidified it for me. As cute as she was, there was no spark, no depth to our conversation, and no fireworks whatsoever. I really felt she didn't care for me in the slightest, so I didn't bother to call her afterward. Shortly thereafter, Hedy would enroll in the nursing program at San Diego State and be away from home for the first time.

The next time I saw Hedy was two summers later when we next met up at a dance. College had opened her up, and we actually had some great conversation that night. I called her the next day to try to spend some time with her before she went back for her junior year. Over the course of that week, I kept leaving messages, but she never returned my call. She had forgotten to tell me one important detail: she had changed her phone number. Thinking a girl should never be the one to call a guy at such an early courtship phase, she never called me. With spite in our souls, she wrote me off and I wrote her off—"*Hasta la vista, baby.*" Two years went by before we would speak to each other again.

It was soon 1987 and I was attending California State University of Long Beach (CSULB) and studying music. My parents were supportive of my drumming, but they were also wise enough to instill in me the importance of having something to fall back on. Dad made me realize I was limiting myself with a music degree. I took his advice and changed majors from music to business instead. A business degree was general enough to apply to any number of industries, I felt. If Dad had his way, I would've become a priest. I had no idea where that was coming from, but it was the last thing on my mind. I didn't even like going to Sunday Mass. I know Dad meant well, but he was definitely off the mark.

Growing up to the music of the '70s and '80s, and with each of the Beatles doing their own solo projects during those years, I don't recall hearing much about the Beatles in my youth. In my last two years of college, I had been playing drums in an original rock group called The Trust. With a singer/songwriter, guitarist, bassist, and drummer, we were a solid four-piece group that blended rhythm and blues with rock and a smidgeon of country and pop. Our bassist was Portuguese and loved to talk about anything, but especially music. His name was Peter, and I came to admire his musical style of playing the bass as well as his deep appreciation for all types of music, including jazz, salsa, rock, classical, and world music. Although I certainly knew who the Beatles were and was familiar with their music, sadly enough I didn't own any of their albums. Peter was always telling stories about the Fab Four and the different ways they recorded songs in the studio, which I found fascinating. The more he spoke about them, the more curious I became.

I went out and bought a few of their records. As the needle worked its way across the vinyl, I realized I knew every song. Up until that point, while I could attribute most of their popular songs to them, I thought their other songs were sung by other '60s bands. I kept saying, "This is the Beatles too?" Song after song, I realized how ignorant I was about their music. This music was fantastic! Typically, on any given album there are several songs (if not most) that could be considered throwaway songs. As I listened to the Beatles' albums, I realized every song was a gem.

And so in great part to Peter, my love and appreciation of the Beatles began. Coincidentally, the entire catalogue of the Beatles was being released on CD for the very first time. They were released one at a time starting with *Please Please Me*, then *Meet the Beatles*, then *Beatles For Sale*, and so on. I would buy each CD the very first day it came out and play it over and over. I kept waiting for a bad song to come on, and I'm still waiting. The fact that they could produce so many quality songs in such a short span of time was astonishing. The more I read and learned about those Beatles years, I realized how utterly amazing it was that they had time to create such great songs amidst touring the world, doing interviews and photo shoots, filming movies, recording singles, re-recording their songs in different languages, and so on. Their schedules were maddening, yet the quality of their music kept getting better.

When I heard side two, track one of *Abbey Road* again, there it was: "One, two, three, four, five, six, seven—all good children go to heaven." Twelve years of Catholic school and countless homilies on how to live one's life were once again summed up in those last six words of that verse. For my own sake, I simply substituted one word for another: "All good *people* go to heaven."

Chapter 2

Ticket To ride

A few months before I graduated with my college degree, my parents had an announcement. As a graduation gift, they asked if I would like to go to Europe. How cool would that be? I had never really given it much thought, but it certainly seemed like a great adventure. They said they would pay for my airfare and a Eurail train pass for three months if I wanted to stay there that long, provided I could get by on my own funds to pay for food and lodging. They said many college students went to Europe after graduation with a backpack and stayed in youth hostels, so it wouldn't cost that much to get by day to day.

We were discussing it in the kitchen when my friend Matt had just come home. Matt was due to graduate with me. When I told him about my parents' gift, his eyes lit up. He was excited by the idea and wanted to join me. Matt lived most of his life as one big adventure. At the age of seventeen, he had a huge party at his parents' house while they were out of town. When they found out, they booted him out on his own. He had done pretty well supporting himself along the way. Matt had been living with us in my parents' home now for several months, and the arrangement was going very well. Most tenants have dozens of house rules they must abide by. My dad just had four rules for Matt if he was to live under our roof: No girls; no parties; rent is due on the first; and in case you forgot, see Rule No. 1.

I had known Matt since high school. We had dozens of mutual friends. We started hanging out more often after we both attended the same colleges together. With dark blonde hair, bluish eyes, and cheerful demeanor, Matt was hard not to like and could talk his way out of almost anything. Quite social, funny, and a bit mischievous, he didn't take himself too seriously and had this inner kid who was often prevalent in his nature. Always fun and the life of the party, he was one of the few friends I have who actually enjoyed, and even sought to engage, adults in conversation as often as he did his teenage peers. I was polite around my parents' friends, but Matt seemed to thoroughly enjoy engaging the older crowd.

Matt and I thought about how great it would be to travel together to Ireland, Paris, Germany, Spain, Italy, and all over Europe without a care in the world. I was happy Matt was going to join me. We started working like crazy to save up enough to cover our day-to-day costs for food, lodging, taxi fares, and miscellaneous travel expenses. Selling door-to-door was simple mathematics. The more doors I knocked on, the more money I could make. For my college years, I sold service station coupon books for routine car maintenance all over Los Angeles. Door-to-door sales made a good part-time living for me, and so for the next several months,

I stepped it up and knocked on as many doors as I could, knowing it was simply a numbers game.

We graduated with bachelor's degrees in late May 1989, Matt in political science and I in business. Shortly thereafter, Matt and I were packing and preparing for our European adventure. Of course, when packing for a four-month trip, there is so much you want to bring. After I laid out my favorite shirts, shorts, sweatshirt, etc., on my bed, I stuffed everything I could into my backpack. Then I realized I'd have to be carrying this weight around a continent. I hadn't yet packed half the clothes and I could barely zip the pack shut. I knew then I needed to simplify in a big way.

We left on June 4, the day of the Tiananmen Square massacre in Beijing. I woke up to the news showing tanks rolling down the streets of Beijing and democracy supporters fighting to survive. It is said that hundreds, if not thousands, of innocent civilians died that day. I felt a little guilty for having the freedom to embark on such a liberating trip while such oppression was happening elsewhere in the world.

Working at British Airways, Matt could fly for free, so I flew on a different airline, but we arrived in London the same day. It was the first time away from family and friends for such an extended period of time. Being together with Matt gave me some level of comfort knowing it would be harder to get into trouble with the two of us—or maybe it would be easier, knowing Matt. Time would certainly tell. Matt was there to greet me when I flew in to Heathrow. He had arranged for us to stay a few days with some acquaintances in Surrey, a beautiful countryside area south of London. The house was simple but very charming and full of antiques. Finding out it had been built in the sixteenth century was surreal for a Southern California kid who thought that something from 1950 was historic.

Matt and I in York, England.

Matt had a few friends we stayed with throughout England. And where there were no friends, we found hostels—cheap rooms with not-so-comfortable beds. After London, we headed up to York, then Hull, then up to Edinburgh, Scotland, where we took in the beautiful castle and historic city. From there we figured we should see if, in fact, the Loch Ness monster did exist. We went to Inverness, Scotland, and visited the famed lake where Nessie is said to swim about. Nessie kept under the water while we were there, but we enjoyed the famous Urquhart Castle adjacent to the lake and climbed up its tower. Neither of us had been so far north before and delighted in the long summer days when the sun sets just before midnight.

From Scotland, it was our plan to work our way back down the interior of the country by train and end up in Liverpool. There were two reasons we would go to Liverpool. First, Ireland was our next destination, and Liverpool is the closest port from which you can catch a ferry to Dublin, just across the Irish Sea. We were anxious to toast a Guinness, see ancient druid ruins, and take in the beautiful green hillsides that one imagines in Ireland. The other reason for our trip to Liverpool was because the greatest band to ever grace the planet hailed from there...The Beatles!

At 7 p.m., Matt and I arrived in Liverpool. Unlike other cities we'd been to so far in England, this one didn't have a youth hostel. We had no idea where we would spend the night. As we disembarked the train, we grabbed our backpacks. We walked with little confidence beyond the train station and entered the sketchy streets of Liverpool, not quite knowing where to go. We were much further south and wouldn't have the luxury of daylight-till-midnight as we had up in Scotland. It was already dusk, and we had less than an hour of light left.

We quickly realized this was hardly a tourist town, and were greeted with looks of bewilderment. We hadn't walked more than three blocks before a middle-aged woman stopped us and asked us, "What are you doing here?" She had no reluctance to tell us that the town was not safe and to be careful. Some welcome. For the first time in nearly two weeks of travel around England, we felt fearful. We kept walking. Another younger woman passed us, and knowing very well we were not locals by our backpacks and colorful Hawaiian shirts from some secondhand store in Southern California, she told us to watch where we went. Younger boys across the street made wisecracks to each other at our expense.

After some distance, we saw a familiar sight: Kentucky Fried Chicken. Being hungry from the long trip from Scotland, we stopped in to eat. As we sat down, five Liverpudlians in their early twenties entered and sat next to us. They stared at us, and though they were also mocking us, we had difficulty making out what they were saying. Up until this point, we thought the English accent so cute and charming. With their thick accents, we could only make out every fourth word as we tried eavesdropping on whether they planned to rob and kill us there or wait until we were outside. After fifteen tense minutes, they approached us from across their table. They were commenting on our beach shorts and shirts. Once we told them we were from Los Angeles, they seemed to lighten their mood and almost appeared appreciative we were visiting their city. Whatever appeal "L.A." had to these boys, it seemed to be a positive. They continued to ask us all kinds of questions about living there. Once we gained their confidence and fooled them into thinking we were "cool," we were able to walk out knowing they were not going to harm us.

We walked the streets looking for bed-and-breakfasts, hotels—anything to get us off the street—only to find them full. Darkness was falling fast, and then we were told to try the local YMCA. I'm not sure if any of downtown Liverpool is nice after dark. Perhaps it's changed since, but this was a seedy area, and there weren't many people walking around the streets, which made it a bit eerie. Thank goodness for the YMCA—we found it and finally felt safe. It wasn't much, but we each had a bed, and it was comfortable, and it was just for one night.

So we were now in Liverpool, the Beatles' birthplace. The next morning, we located the office that provided van tours of the city and were all set to take the Beatles tour. I didn't realize it then, but this would be the day that would spark my spiritual conversion. This visit to Liverpool began my faith journey and would lead me to my personal encounter with the Mother of God. It would reintroduce me to Jesus in a way I never would have thought possible.

We visited the sights of Liverpool from the perspectives of John, Paul, George, and Ringo. In a shuttle van driven by an elderly lady, we drove around sunny Liverpool, and she pointed out some of the famous sights related to the Beatles. Driving around the shelter in the middle of a roundabout, we saw a fire station and barbershop made famous by Paul in Penny Lane. We also drove by John's childhood stomping ground, known as Strawberry Fields, which was actually a Salvation Army home for children. We took in Saint Peter's Church, where Paul and John first met when John's group, the Quarrymen, had been performing at a church function. Listening to the songs of the Beatles on her tape-cassette stereo, we drove to each of the homes where the Beatles grew up.

On the way, as we were driving up a highway, our driver pointed out a large, round, concrete church to our left. She recommended visiting there if any of us had time, as it was one of the better-known landmarks in Liverpool. After having been inside Westminster Abbey, we thought it would be hard to top such a cathedral as that. I didn't give it much of a thought.

After the tour, we enjoyed the downtown hustle and bustle of Liverpool and frequented Matthews Street, where the Fab Four drew thousands of youngsters to the infamous Cavern Club, where they got their start. By early afternoon there were hoards of people milling around: businessmen in suits, women shopping, and others frequenting their favorite pub for lunch. Later in the afternoon, we found ourselves at a local pub taking in a pint of something along with some fish and chips. Our plans were to take the ferry that evening to Dublin, which would take us away from Liverpool and onto the green shores of Ireland where the people greet you like a day of sunshine.

It would be three hours before we could board the ferry. Sitting on that dock made us feel like cargo, and we were bored. Matt said, "Hey, Dennis, remember that church the tour guide said to check out? It's walking distance from here. We may as well kill the time." I went along.

Before long, we were gazing upon the Cathedral of Christ the King. Matt and I approached the large church and concluded that the architect must have been the same one who designed Space Mountain at Disneyland. A large round mass of white concrete with a tall spire in the middle evoked the contemporary space theme. At least that's how I saw it. Inside, the altar was in the middle of the church with the pews circling around it, going up many rows to the sides of the large structure, where there were numerous side chapels. Stained glass let in rays of light. It was much more beautiful on the inside than on the outside. As we gazed at all the side chapels and viewed the statues and many candles, there were only a few other people inside this Catholic church, which stood out in such a Protestant country. I was reminded from history that before King Henry VIII, England was an entirely Catholic country. It is interesting that the present-day Church of England owes its beginnings to Henry who, in 1534, formed the church after the pope would not allow him to divorce his wife, Catherine of Aragon. Henry's anger erupted and he set out to separate all of England from Rome, and Catholic persecutions began in earnest.

After a few minutes of walking around the church, Matt came up to me and said, "They are about to start Mass in the side chapel over there. Want to go?"

Since we had not been to Mass in a couple of weeks, I said, "Sure, why not?" Matt was one of the few friends I had who wasn't raised Catholic, but he had recently gone through the RCIA (Rite of Christian Initiation for Adults) process at our home church in Redondo Beach.

Matt and I ventured into a little side chapel while waiting for Mass to begin. There were ten small pews with about five other people sitting patiently. A priest came out, and we both enjoyed the fact that this cut-to-the-chase Mass only lasted about twenty-five minutes. As he said the closing prayer and blessed us, I have to admit my mind was elsewhere. I was thinking about the fact that I would be in Ireland by the next morning, a place I had longed to visit.

When Mass was over, we walked out of the pew toward the exit of the church. The priest who had just said Mass came up to us and said, "Boys, I need to speak with you for a moment. Wait right here, I'll be right back."

Off he went with another individual, and we stood motionless, looking at each other, feeling like we had done something wrong. We stood in the aisle outside the side chapel, which bordered the main seating area of the church, for several minutes. We weren't sure whether to leave or not, since we thought we may have upset him. Maybe we genuflected on the wrong knee? Perhaps our laidback Southern California appearance with shorts and T-shirts were too casual? Or perhaps it was my red, white, and blue tennis shoes?

After some time, the priest came back, and without any emotion on his face, he said, "Boys, come with me." With our hearts picking up some tempo, he silently led us through a side door of the church, down a set of stairs, and along a narrow hallway. We entered through a door into a large room with a table in the middle, some chairs, and cabinets that contained various church supplies. He told us to sit down and that he would be back in a moment. As he left the room, Matt and I once again looked at each other and whispered, "What is going on here?"

After what seemed like an hour—though it was really much less—a nun walked in, went to one of the shelves, and picked out a book. As she was walking back, she looked at us. Not a word was said, but she did sport a little smile. That relieved us somewhat, but maybe she didn't know what we had done to upset this priest. Or perhaps she did know and was smiling because she knew of the punishment that was due. In such tense moments, the mind has a way of plotting a thousand outcomes. After the nun had left, more minutes passed. Then the priest walked back in and without fully entering the room said, "Boys, please come this way." We got up from our folding chairs and followed the priest back down the long, narrow corridor. We went down a different route and entered into what appeared to be the rectory, which seemed to be attached to the church. We were silently following him as he led us into his office, where he asked us to sit down.

He asked us if we were thirsty and if we would care for some apple juice. It was at this point I felt he might not be so bad and that maybe I was getting all worked up over nothing. If he were angry with us, why would he offer us juice? He came back with the juice, and he said, "You're Americans, aren't you?"

"Do we stand out that much?"

He replied, "When you received the Eucharist, you said aye-men, rather than ah-men, like we say over here." My heart was beginning to slow down, and this middle-aged priest came across as very pleasant and seemed quite interested in Matt and me. We told him we were traveling Europe, having just graduated from college, and we were planning on seeing most of the European countries over the next four months.

We continued to make small talk, and then the priest began to tell us of a place we had not heard of before. It was called Medjugorje and was located in what was then Yugoslavia. He said he had just returned from his second trip there and reported to us how the Blessed Virgin Mary had been appearing to six children there in the church they attend. I was astounded when he said they actually see her every day and that this had been occurring for the previous eight years! He went on to say that people were visiting there from all over the world in great numbers. The local villagers were gracious enough to put people up in their homes for a small fee instituted by the communist government. He said that we could get to Medjugorje by train from Austria, and that since we were so close to this phenomenal event, we should not pass up the opportunity to go while making our travels throughout Europe.

We had many questions: "How come we didn't hear about this before?" "Why a communist country?" "What is Mary saying to these kids?" "How do we know this is not a hoax?"

The priest assured us that after a trip there, all our questions would be answered. In fact, he said that two other Americans had visited his church about a year before, and after hearing his testimony said they would try to make time for a few days in Medjugorje. A couple of months passed, and then he received a postcard from them. They had spent not several days, but several weeks there! It seemed that something of significance was taking place there, which might be worth checking out.

As we were getting ready to leave his office to catch our ferry to Ireland, the priest grabbed both our hands and, with a firm grasp, looked us straight in the eyes. His visage seemed to penetrate my soul when he said with a soft-spoken voice, "Boys, you must go to Medjugorje!" This seemed almost more of a command than a request, especially coming from a priest. For the next six weeks, I could not forget his words or the manner in which they were delivered. Whether I was lying in the bed of a youth hostel in Norway before falling asleep, eating a sausage in a courtyard in Munich, or hiking up a mountain in Gimmerwald, Switzerland, the priest, whom I remember only as Father John, would come to me with that command. His words seemed to lead me to that place of beckoning.

Playing soccer with Irish kids on the Dingle Peninsula.

Matt and I subsequently traveled to Ireland, France, Belgium, Holland, Denmark, Germany, Sweden, and Norway before our paths separated. Before leaving on this trip, Matt had applied to teach English in Japan. He wasn't so sure he would be accepted, but he was, and they wanted him to start very soon. We didn't know it at the time, but Japan would become his new home.

After an amazing dinner overlooking the harbor in Oslo the night before, Matt and I said our good-byes on a hillside outside of a youth hostel the next morning. We had some great times together, experienced some fantastic sights, and made some friends along the way. I was so grateful for his companionship, and would miss him now that I would be a solo adventurer. I made my way south through Germany again, then Switzerland, and then to Austria, where I found myself in Vienna.

Boat ride through a Norwegian Wooded fiord.

Perhaps someday I'll write a separate book about my travels throughout Western Europe before and after Matt left. I met some interesting people along the way—both tourists like me, and locals who opened up their hearts and homes to me. As I would meet people either at a restaurant, a youth hostel, a cathedral, museum, or on the street, I'd often ask them if they had heard of Medjugorje. I never came across anyone who said they had. When I explained what the priest in Liverpool had told me, they seemed genuinely interested. As this would lead to a casual conversation on spirituality, I would find out that most people I met along the way weren't religious at all. Most seemed to be agnostic or atheist, despite Europe being a predominantly Christian continent. As I said, these people were kind enough to buy me meals, drinks, and put me up in their homes, so their level of hospitality was that of a close family member. I had no prejudice toward them, and they treated me in the most Christian-like manner without even knowing it. I just couldn't understand how people so gracious and caring couldn't believe in God and see the beauty of his creation around them. Furthermore, almost every city I was in seemed to have these tremendous churches on every street corner, yet they were like empty pieces of art one could admire passing by on the street. What had happened to this continent?

Hiking around the Matterhorn. Zermatt, Switzerland.

It was now August 2, 1989. I acquired a visa for Yugoslavia from the embassy in Vienna. In the back of my mind, even though I had the visa, I still told myself there was nothing forcing me to go to Medjugorje. I was nervous about going there only because it was a communist country. Even if I didn't see Mary and what the priest had said was all a hoax, I'd still enjoy the adventure of it all—as long as I came out alive. But perhaps I shouldn't go, I thought. I had the visa, and buyer's remorse was setting in.

After checking out of the hostel, I went to the Vienna train station to see how I would find this little town where Mary was appearing. Growing up, I had never heard much about what goes on in a communist country, other than a lot of oppression and persecution. I pictured a communist country in black and white, as if there was no color there. It was always overcast and grey, and people waited in long lines for food staples. Yes, it was a childish vision, for not many others crept in my mind over the years to dispute what I imagined. It wouldn't surprise me if there were communist police on every corner, ready to take away any unsuspecting foreigner who might be a spy. I was anxious with excitement, yet feared the unknown.

I wasn't sure how I would find this place, but I would give it a try. I had always placed some degree of trust in God to protect me and get me where I needed to go. He certainly had not let me down on this trip thus far. I began to recollect my thoughts: "Let's see, the priest said the name was Meshagoria or something like that, right?" At the train station, I noticed an information booth. I was confident the person attending the booth could help me catch the necessary trains to get there. These booths had been quite handy in past weeks as the staff working in them would point out the exact train to take and note down the departing and arriving times. The system ran like clockwork—literally, when a train arrived at 3:42, it arrived at 3:42, not a minute before or after. An upgrade to first class was not much more money over a three-month Eurail pass than a second-class pass, so I had been riding in luxury in first class cabins all the way. Most importantly, in this high summer season of traveling, I never had a problem with the first class section being full, which was the case for those sorry backpackers with a second-class ticket.

Up until this point, it did not take much to figure how to get from one European city to the next. With the help of these booths and my *Let's Go Europe* travel guide, it was a breeze. Matt and I had never planned too much in advance. We knew we had wanted to start in Britain, get up to Scandinavia, and then work our way down south. We made our plans almost on a day-to-day basis, figuring we would spend a few days here, a couple of days there, and so on. There was always room for flexibility. I left the planning for getting to Medjugorje until the last day of my departure city, because that was what I was used to doing. Now in Vienna, I would for the first time encounter a problem finding the way to my destination. The fact that I could not properly spell the village's name and that it was in a communist country did not help.

The person working at the booth could not make out what I was saying and said there was no city with that name in Yugoslavia. I told her that the Mother of Christ was appearing there, that people from all over the world were apparently going there, and surely someone must have come to her before with this. She said no. Now I was at a crossroads. I was not going to just take a train and not know where I would end up. I knew finding people in a communist country who spoke English would not be as common as in Western Europe. I had no listing of hotels or youth hostels east of Austria. I might as well have been going to another planet.

I thought about this problem in the train station as I walked away from the information booth. The priest in Liverpool had really sounded convincing. I told him I would go there almost out of obligation, or so it seemed. Maybe he was out of his mind. Nobody I ran into seemed to know about this place. Why hadn't I heard about it on *Oprah* or *60 Minutes*? Shouldn't this have been front-page news in all the world's papers?

There was a lot of curiosity stirring inside me about this place. I'd always thought priests to be pretty credible. On the other hand, this would make a great joke if you really wanted to steer someone the wrong way. I decided to believe his story. It seemed too good to pass up, given I was kind of in the neighborhood. It was at this moment I decided to call on God. I said a little prayer, "God, if you want me to go to this place called Meshagoria, you are going to have to help me here. I've tried. If it is meant to be that I go, you've got to show me the way."

I was impatient now. Circling the interior of the train station, my mind raced with thoughts of how I would get there. A thought occurred to me. A map! A map was what I needed, of course. I walked back over to the information booth and asked if they had a map of Yugoslavia. Again, she said no. I thought this too strange. Trains depart from Vienna to Yugoslavia all the time, yet the person who is supposed to have all the information did not even carry a map? I asked her, "Where can I get a map?"

She shrugged, and in her broken English, replied, "Perhaps bookstore," and she pointed over my shoulder. I turned around, and across the station was indeed a bookstore.

I walked over and went inside a bookstore filled with newspapers, magazines, and books of all kinds as well as various souvenirs.

I looked all over but could not find any maps. After about five minutes, my patience was wearing thin, and I began to walk toward the exit. Near the exit aisle, I found what I was looking for. Maps of Vienna, Salzburg, Austria, Germany, and then there it was—Yugoslavia! There was only one in the compartment. I unfolded it, and in the end, it was about four feet tall and five feet across! The entire country of Yugoslavia was filled with dizzying small print. There must have been half-a-million names on that map! How in the world would I find a place I did not even know how to spell? I glanced at the multitude of names, most of which were un-pronounceable to me. My eyes gazed up, down, across, slowly and then faster. There was no way I was going to find the town this way. I could feel my blood pressure begin to elevate. It would have been so easy to just throw it down, walk away, and head off to Italy or Greece and take in their topless beaches. Wait, scratch the topless beaches. I remember the ones Matt and I visited in Sweden and Denmark. The only girls topless seemed to be senior citizens, and you can imagine the effects of decades of gravity on braless bosoms. Include the hairy armpits, and we're pretty far off from "sexy".

For some reason, I felt compelled to get to Medjugorje now. I was not going to be detoured by the small fact that I had no idea where I was going. It was a silly game, yet I persisted. I checked to see if there was any index or alphabetical listing of cities or town with grid numbers to follow. No such luck. I was at my wit's end, but I thought I'd give it one more shot. I took the unfolded map, which had my arms spread five feet apart, and went to the cashier where there were a couple of people waiting in line to purchase their items. I was not the type to go out of turn or cut in front of someone, but my patience was all but gone. I laid the large map on the counter and asked the cashier, "Do you know where Meshagoria would be on this map?"

"No English," he replied.

I pointed down to the map, and as my index finger circled the million names, I said the word several times, "Meshagoria, Meshagoria, have you heard of it?"

Starting to get upset at me now, the cashier replied, "No, no English," and motioned me aside so he could take care of the customers waiting on my left.

Just as I was ready to throw in the towel, the lady to my left who I had cut in front of spoke up, "Medjugorje? Medjugorje? Is that what you are looking for?" I wanted to kiss her just for speaking English!

With excitement, I said, "Meshagoria! Do you know where it is? I'm not sure how to spell it or where it's located."

With no condemnation in her tone for having just been cut off, she glanced at the map for a few seconds, then politely said, "I believe it is somewhere around here," and she circled an area with her finger that was perhaps the size of the palm of my hand. That narrowed it down to about one hundred names. Now I was sure I would find it. I thanked her and stepped aside and began searching for any word that sounded similar to Meshagoria. Within moments, I found what I thought was the place. Because the lady was still finishing her purchase, I went over as she was about to exit the bookstore. I pointed to Medjugorje on the map and said, "Is that it, you think?"

With a little hesitation, her eyes looked around the map, and she finally said with total confidence, "Yes, that is it."

The chances of such a thing happening are slim. It had to be the will of God. I went back to the information booth, and now that they knew where this place was on a map, they were able to assist me by looking at the train schedules. It was located in Bosnia-Herzegovina, which was about an hour outside of the city of Mostar. My train connections were mapped out on a piece of paper with the arrival times. Now that it was about 6 p.m., I had to wait until 11:15 p.m. before the train left Vienna.

I went to exchange some money. Fifty dollars bought me one million Yugoslavian dinars. Even if imaginary, it felt good to be a millionaire. I sat at the station and waited with anticipation for the train to depart. The train would travel through the night. I happened to be in a cabin with two Belgian girls from Antwerp traveling to Yugoslavia as well. They made me feel a little more comfortable. Young ladies actually do go to a communist country on holiday, with no male bodyguards needed. That was good to know. Their English was flawless, so we chatted some of the way. It was difficult to sleep on the train, and at least on two occasions before we arrived at our connecting station, the train would stop and military men armed with guns would board the train and come by each cabin to check our passports and visas. This had not happened in Western Europe. If it was meant to intimidate us, it worked. These stops would usually occur just as I was nodding off to sleep—another reason I didn't sleep much.

We arrived at about six or seven in the morning, just after the sun had risen at the Strizivojna Vrpolje train station. I had to wait several hours for the next train to arrive. I lay on a bench and, using my backpack as a pillow, tried to grab a nap. The station was quite dirty in comparison to those in Western Europe. It appeared to be a small town. There were some mountains in the distance, and the landscape was dry and barren. As the morning wore on, I begged God for a breeze. The heat became unbearable until my departure train arrived.

The train arrived in a cloud of dust packed with people. As the doors opened, I waited, as is customary, for people to exit first before boarding. They were shoulder to shoulder crammed inside. Nobody got off the train. My Eurail pass did not work in Yugoslavia for first class, so I entered what looked like a cattle car. I boarded the train and traversed back and forth through a couple of cars, squeezing between hot, sweaty bodies and trying to find a place to sit. It was standing room only. This spoiled little American was not used to such chaos and congestion. The train cars were filled with cigarette smoke, which I happened to be allergic to, and the only air conditioning was the open windows with hardly a breeze. Passengers disregarded the signs everywhere depicting a cigarette with a red line crossed through it. I must have been the only one not smoking. Everyone spoke in a language I could not understand. Spotting foreign travelers was usually pretty easy, and it would have been nice to be able to speak English with someone. No such luck on this train—all locals. I thought I would see Europeans and others wearing T-shirts that said "Medjugorje or Bust," but nobody seemed like they were going where I was headed.

The train seemed a hundred years old. It was certainly not the comfortable ride you would experience in Western Europe. The seats were falling apart and paint was chipping, and that was only where enough dirt had rubbed off so you could see the paint. I managed to find the only place where I could stand, which was where two cars connected. I wasn't exactly standing with one foot on each train car, but more to one side and on the end. This happened to be right in front of the bathroom— although calling it that is actually a stretch, because a "bathroom" implies certain features that were not evident there. The stench was putrid, and it taught me why nobody else had chosen this exact spot. Still, there were bodies all around me. One lady was sitting on a wooden crate filled with some chickens. A scruffy, elderly man across from me stood next to his three big bags of rice stacked on top of each other. He motioned, inviting me to sit, but I politely refused. This would have taken me a few feet further away from the bathroom, but I felt like standing. Well, honestly, I wanted to sit, but just not next to him.

I imagined there must have been a door on this bathroom at some point, but no longer. The bathroom appeared smaller than an airplane restroom and was a filthy mess, to say the least. It was so bad that no reasonable person would dare go in there. This bathroom would test the bladders of all on board like they never thought possible. There was no toilet, but simply a hole in the floor through which you could see the blur of the tracks passing below. The wet floor provided evidence that, due to the gentle rocking motion of the train, not everyone had made their target.

I felt sick to my stomach between the chickens, the smoke, and the stench of the bathroom. Shifting my weight from one foot to the other, I stood in that spot for four hours before we reached Sarajevo, and I thought I would die before ever reaching Medjugorje. The dry and barren countryside began to change as we neared Sarajevo. Hills and mountains sprang up on either side. The scenery turned from brown grass to green trees filling the countryside, and it became quite visually pleasant aside from my immediate surroundings. Lakes, rivers, and forests appeared, and as the landscape unfolded, so did a natural beauty that I didn't expect. My mood lifted. We stopped at the station in Sarajevo, where I switched to another train that would take me to Mostar.

Noticing that second class on this train was also overflowing, I decided to do what Matt would have done. I went to first class, and with the utmost confidence, I quickly flashed my Eurail pass to the attendant while looking in his eyes, and with a huge smile said, "How are you today, my friend?" I kept walking past him to a vacant seat. It worked. What a break. The cabin capacity for eight people only held two other men, so I had plenty of room to stretch my legs. Now it was late in the afternoon, and I hadn't eaten anything all day and I regretted not having gotten enough water between trains in Sarajevo. This was before some genius realized he could bottle tap water and sell it for $2 apiece. I remembered that I had some crackers left over, so I dipped them in the honey jar I'd been given by an Austrian I met a couple of weeks before. He had let me stay with his family on their farm outside of Salzburg for several days. It only served to remind me that I was a long, long way from home, and the distance was increasing with every taste of honey. I figured that would tide me over until I got to Mostar.

I had no idea where I was going to stay in Mostar. I wasn't sure how big or small of a city it was. Would there be any youth hostels or hotels? I wasn't sure. I had trusted God to always lead me in the right direction, and it was in these moments when I had no other options before me that I could not help but place my trust in him. Other than having to sit next to a stinking toilet and hold my breath for four hours, he had not let me down so far. Perhaps I deserved it. It was on this leg of the journey that I really began to reflect on what Father John had told me in Liverpool. The butterflies fluttered in my stomach as I began to think about where I was going. If it were true, I began to anticipate how historic this would be. I had never heard of Mary appearing to anyone before in my lifetime.

As the train moved past this greener part of Yugoslavia, I began to recall what my mother had told me about Our Lady of Guadalupe. I was twelve years old when my parents returned from a vacation to Mexico City. My mom gave me some Mexican candy that was like rock candy and told me of their trip to the Basilica of Our Lady of Guadalupe. She told me the story of how

Juan Diego had been asked by the Virgin Mary to build a church in her honor. To prove to the local bishop this was true, Juan carried a tilma full of roses, normally out of bloom, from the countryside all the way to the bishop's residence. When he dropped the roses on the floor, the image of Mary appeared on his cloak. It was this very tilma my parents had seen in the church that eventually was built to honor Our Lady. Mom went on to explain that this occurred 450 years ago and this same tilma, which normally had a lifespan of about twenty years, is still there today behind bullet-proof glass.

I sat in awe when Mom showed me a picture of an iron cross bent backward due to a bomb that was detonated inside the cathedral by some deranged individual who tried to blow up the tilma. Though the windows were blown out and the damage to the church was quite severe, the tilma was not scratched. I was a believer in Our Lady of Guadalupe from then on. As a daydreaming child of twelve, I thought it would be so cool to have Mary appear in my lifetime. As the train rolled along and I thought back on Our Lady of Guadalupe, it dawned on me that maybe she was appearing in my lifetime and I was going to Medjugorje to see her! It was as if my childhood dream had come true.

On the train to Mostar, I asked the man sitting across from me if he spoke any English. He said he knew a little bit. I asked him if he or the man sitting next to him had heard of Medjugorje. At first he said no, but when I told him that Mary, the Mother of Jesus, was supposedly appearing there, he nodded his head. He went on to say in broken English that he had heard of that place, but he hadn't been there. He said that many people have traveled there. I was surprised that not everyone in this country knew about this place, and moreover that they wouldn't have visited there as well. I couldn't understand why, if such a thing were taking place, the whole world wouldn't be descending upon this place and be spreading the word.

It was nearing eight in the evening when the train pulled into Mostar. The sun was beginning to set. I was hungry and extremely thirsty. It would be several more months before communism in this part of the world would crumble along with the Berlin wall, allowing many Eastern Europeans to flee into the West to escape decades of oppression. Though Yugoslavia was the most Westernized of the Eastern nations, it was still a communist country. I didn't notice any other tourists or backpackers on my train. These were all local people who filed out onto the station platform. I felt isolated in this foreign place. I felt a bit scared—like the time I was with Matt in Liverpool when we got off the train in a rough part of town, but this time I was alone.

As I stepped off the train, I was looking due west, where I could see in the distance many buildings in the twilight. This appeared to be a good-sized city. I stood for a minute with my backpack on, watching as everyone departed from the train to greet waiting relatives and head off to wherever they were going. I just stood there, not knowing where to go. I noticed a large lady, probably in her late forties, approaching the last few people exiting the train. I watched as she greeted a couple of men traveling alone and spoke to them in her native Croatian. They shook their heads as to say no, and she would look for another prospect.

Within a short time, there were only a couple of other passengers around the platform. This same lady came rushing over to me. I decided it was time to stop looking like an idiot tourist and make like I knew where I was going. Of course I figured the backpack was a dead giveaway. Nonetheless, I began to walk in the opposite direction. She came up from behind me and grabbed my arm to turn me around toward her. She was speaking in an aggressive tone, but I could not make out what she was saying. I wasn't sure if she needed help, or if she was a beggar, or what. Then, as she was still holding my arm and looking me in the eyes, she said the few English words she knew.

She put her index finger on my chest and said, "You! You! Me! Me! Me!" pointing her finger back at herself and saying, "Sleep, sleep! You sleep me, you sleep me!"

At this point, I became nervous, not so much because I thought her to be a communist prostitute, but because she was still holding my arm with some force, and she was three times my size. I stared at her dumbly and shook my head and said, "No, no, thank you, no, sorry, I only speak English."

She was determined to get through to me. She said in a louder tone the same words, and then pointed down the platform where a teenage boy was going up to the last person exiting a couple of train cars down. She said, "Son, son," and then pointed to her chest. I could figure that out and thought how disgusting that a boy would help lure people to sleep with his own mother. What a sick society this was. I thought things were bad in the States, but this was outrageous. A thought crossed my mind to just get back on the train and wait for it to take off to the next city. I wanted to get away, but this heavy-set lady would not let go of me. She then placed her hands together as if to pray and then put them to the side of her cheek as she cocked her head a little to that side. She then repeated the words, "Sleep, sleep...you sleep!"

It was then I put it together. I figured she must have a hotel or something and this was how she drummed up business. I looked at her son as he walked toward us since he had no takers. She saw that some of the fear and hesitation was leaving my face, and she began to smile, knowing I had finally understood what she meant. She pointed across the train track to a hill with some houses. As she pointed she said, "Home, home...you sleep me home." I figured since I didn't have any other options, I might as well go with this lady and her son.

I wasn't sure if she would kidnap me and cut me into a dozen pieces or what. Was she a nice communist or a mean communist? Truthfully, if her son had not been there, I probably would have blown her off and ran away. He seemed innocent enough, and he extended his hand and said, "Tony, Tony." I shook his hand and gave them my name. The three of us walked over the tracks and along a dirt trail. It went up toward the hill. After passing some houses, we came to theirs. It had two stories and an outdoor patio where there were some chairs circling a table that sat beneath grape vines strung across horizontal wires.

She motioned for me to sit down, and she seemed pleased that she had a person to rent a room for the night. She patted her hand on her tummy and asked in Croatian if I was hungry. Though I did not understand the Croatian, I did understand the sign language. I nodded, and off she went inside the house to prepare supper. I had only eaten some crackers and honey the whole day, and I was starving. Out came her sons: Tony, the oldest at sixteen, and his younger brothers Josef and Alex. They greeted me and sat next to me and smiled. Each of them had an olive complexion with dark wavy hair.

Within several minutes, a thin, young girl named Nela appeared. She was sixteen and lived a couple of houses over. She had a soft complexion with straight, light brown hair and striking brown eyes. She was a friend of this family and happened to know English very well. We got to talking, and I explained to Nela that I was going to Medjugorje and asked what she knew about it. She had heard much about it, although she had never been there. She was Muslim but mentioned that this family known now to me as the Vrbanec family was Catholic and had been there on many occasions. She told me that a bus would take me to Medjugorje. The bus left several times throughout the day from the train station. It was about an hour-long trip from Mostar. I asked her if she knew the times because I wanted to get there first thing in the morning if possible. She made a few comments to Tony in Croatian, and off he went running down the hill. She told me he would go to the station and bring back the bus schedule for me. What service! I was extremely grateful.

While I was waiting for Tony to return, I was given a shot of homemade plum peppermint schnapps. I obliged, and just then Mrs. Vrbanek came outside from the kitchen with several plates of food. Nela told me the mother's first name was Mira. She had prepared a plate full of wiener-schnitzel (Vienna-style breaded veal cutlets) with accompanying plates of fresh tomatoes and onions, homemade bread and jam, and cooked bell peppers. I thought they were surely going to join me, but she merely set all the food down in front of me, stepped back, and looked at me with a grin. Yes, I was hungry, but this was a meal for four people. I asked Nela if anyone else would join me. She said they had all eaten already and that this was for me. I couldn't believe it. After eighteen hours of miserable travel, this made it all worthwhile.

The home-cooked food tasted so good. Toward the end of my meal, her youngest son came out with a violin. He stood next to my chair and played a couple of songs. Being serenaded—albeit by an eleven-year-old playing his violin while I ate a five-course meal was quite a treat. It was one of the best dining experiences I had ever had. Just when I thought I could not eat any more, Mira brought out another plate full of pastries, along with some Turkish coffee. I really could not eat anything else. They just stared at me with a smile on their faces, and I felt I had to eat one or two so as to not offend her. Though we could not communicate verbally, Mira was pleased that I had eaten most of the food and sampled the dessert. From that point on, she insisted I call her, "Mama."

Tony came back from the bus station and gave me the times the buses left for Medjugorje in the morning. The earliest was 7:00 a.m., which was the one I decided to take. Nela made sure Mira would wake me in plenty of time to take a shower and get ready for the bus. After being treated so well, I wasn't so sure I even wanted to even leave their house. If it wasn't for Nela, it would have been awkward communicating with only charades, so I was grateful she was there. I didn't come this far to be spoiled, though. I felt called to Medjugorje for some reason and knew in my heart that this was something I must check out for myself, even if it meant sacrificing comfort.

I was not going to Medjugorje as a pilgrim or out of devotion of any kind. That is how most travelers go to Medjugorje. Typically, groups of people make the trip as a spiritual journey from their homes, accompanied by a priest or nun if possible. Some go with relatives and friends from their church community. Some go seeking a miracle for someone they know who is ill or handicapped. Others go after having difficulty suffering the loss of a loved one. They feel that Medjugorje can give their hearts the consolation they need. Some go because they realize they have hit an emotional low, and after hearing about the loving presence Medjugorje provides, they hope to piece their lives together and come to terms with their personal struggles. Some go at the urging of someone who has been there before. Of course, I learned all this later—all I knew was that I had been drawn there by the words of a Liverpudlian priest.

People of all ages from different parts of the world travel to Medjugorje, spending weeks, months, and even years planning

for such a trip. Coming from various backgrounds and profes-
sions, they chart out every detail and know how they will get
there and where they will stay. They go as believers and skep-
tics, Catholics or not; many bring their rosaries, their intentions,
their Bibles, holy objects, and most definitely, their faith. They go
to worship God on what they believe is holy ground. They go to
strengthen their spiritual lives. They go hoping their prayers will
be answered and their hearts may be converted to Christ in a way
they have not experienced before. They eagerly anticipate being
blessed to see miracles or at least be present during an apparition.

Yes, people go to Medjugorje for many different reasons. For
most, it is simply to draw closer to God. Looking back, I'm not
sure where I fit in. More than anything, I was a curiosity-seeker.
I was taking a side trip on my European adventure. Though I had
tried to have God in my life, I did not then have what I would
call a "close" relationship with him. The rest of the world seemed
to be caught up in secularism, and I felt comfortable conforming
to that. I wasn't the saintliest person, but I certainly wasn't the
worst sinner either. I figured down the road I would marry, have
a few kids, live in a house with a decent paying job, go to church
on Sunday, and grow old. God is what we have to look forward
to when we died, right? That was pretty much where I stood in
my spiritual life as I spent the eve of my Medjugorje trip with the
Vrbanec family and Nela. Looking back, it was better that I was
alone as I ventured to Medjugorje. For God to work in me the way
he did, I might have had a lesser experience had I gone the route
so many other people did.

Chapter 3

THE MAGICAL MYSTERY TOUR

The next morning, Tony escorted me to the bus station and made sure I got on the right bus. It was summer, and like any teenager, he would have enjoyed sleeping in, but Tony took the time to see me off and I was very grateful. The sparsely filled bus wound its way through Mostar and into the Yugoslavian countryside, which in this period of midsummer was dry and brown. It was obvious I was the only tourist on board. The day was bright. The sun had barely risen from the eastern mountain peaks, but its heat was already strong, and I knew it would be another scorching day. The scenery reminded me of Baja Mexico, with shrubs, short trees and rocky hills. Soon enough, the bus made its way to the little town of Medjugorje. It pulled to a complete stop just over a small bridge on the east side of the village. I exited the bus and strapped on my backpack. I stood still on the side of the road and watched the people scatter into the distance while the bus pulled away.

I was finally here. It was 8 a.m; it was quiet and calm, with the exception of a lone rooster crowing. The sky was as blue as blue could be. I wasn't sure what to expect now that I was here. The town seemed much smaller than I had imagined. I saw homes in the distance beyond the fields, stretching out to the base of the surrounding mountains. I stood alone on the edge of the dusty street, and then I started walking toward a church in the distance, which towered over the smaller houses around it. Could this be the church Father John in Liverpool had talked about? Its twin steeples rose above the main body of the church as if reaching for the sky. Most of the homes were no more than two or three stories tall, so this large structure seemed to be the center of the town. There were no skyscrapers, and this was no modern city. It probably hadn't changed much in a hundred years. The barely paved street was empty—no cars or people. There was stillness. It seemed peaceful, and I began to wonder if anyone lived here at all. I thought maybe I'd see Mary floating around somewhere in the sky. She was nowhere to be seen.

There were shops and several tourist agencies lining the main street, but none were open at this early hour. As I walked, I noticed a young lady through a window standing behind the counter of one such tourist agency. I was happy to see someone from this town, so I pressed closer. The glass door was locked, but as I got closer the lady met my eyes and sensed my need to speak with her and warmly opened the door to let me in. I greeted her, and she said her name was Vera. She was a beautiful girl with bronzed skin, blonde hair, and stunning blue eyes. I wasn't quite sure what to say. "Hey, I'm looking for the Virgin Mary. Do you know where I can find her?"

I told her the bus had just let me off, and I was here because a priest in Liverpool had told me to come. She said that was good, and she welcomed me to her village. I noticed some pictures of Mary behind her on a bulletin board, and I appreciated the fact that she could speak English. After a couple of minutes of small talk, I came out with the question: "Is it true that Mary, the Mother of Christ, is appearing to some children here?" I felt awkward asking such a direct question and wasn't sure what kind of answer I would get.

Vera looked at me and with the utmost conviction said, "Oh, yes, she is."

"What do people do when they come here? What sights do they go and see?" I asked. She said there was a small hill to climb where Mary first appeared, known as Apparition Hill, and the Hill of the Cross, also known as Mount Krizevac. There was Mass every day and plenty of time to pray and fast. I felt that in some way she was trying to keep a secret from me. That priest in Liverpool told me that Mary appeared here every day. If such a thing were true, why wouldn't she tell me where I could see her?

To see if this Father John had been right, I asked Vera, "Is it true that Mary is appearing here every day?"

"Oh yes," she replied, "since 1981. She appears sometimes on the hills at night but always in the early evening in the church choir loft before the Mass."

I pointed in the direction of the church and said, "Which church? That one down the street?"

She tried to restrain her laughter and replied, "Yes, that is the only church here in Medjugorje!" Surreally, it dawned on me what this lady was telling me —that the Virgin Mary appeared in *this* church, which I could see with my own eyes right at this moment, *every day*. Later today she would be *in* that same church!

"My God," I thought, "what if this is actually happening?" This seemed all too weird. Could this be possible?

Then I realized something. I had been a curiosity-seeker up until now, but now I was beginning to see things in a new light. I thought that if this were actually taking place, and the Mother of Jesus Christ was appearing here every day, then I should look at this a little differently. I shouldn't be looking for a "show." It was all too much to take in—that is, if it was authentic. Maybe there was a good explanation for all this. I would allow the events to play out while I was here. I would take Vera's advice and do what there was to do here, and after a couple of days, I would have a clearer idea about what was or wasn't taking place. Vera was kind enough to give me a brief history of the apparitions, and I asked her where I might be able to stay.

She said that since it was the busy season, it would be very difficult to find a room, especially at the last minute. But, she would try. She picked up the telephone, and after I listened to her speaking in Croatian for a minute, she hung up and said someone would be by to take me to a home where I could stay.

Within minutes, a middle-aged man drove up in a small car and motioned to me to get inside, which I did after thanking Vera for her assistance. We couldn't have gone more than a couple of hundred feet when he stopped in front of a house. Speaking no English, he offered to take my backpack. I obliged, and at the front door, an elderly lady wearing a veil and with peace shining in her eyes, welcomed me into her home. The man who had driven me motioned me to go with her. He warmly shook my hand, then waved good-bye. The lady showed me to a room where there were three beds, two of which held two sleeping young men and the other still open for me.

I laid my backpack on the floor and decided to go out and explore the town, and perhaps catch a glimpse of Mary. As I stepped outside and looked around, the twin spires of the church of Saint James seemed to draw me toward them like a magnet. I passed by the souvenir shops and travel agencies that lined the main road leading to the church. As I came up to the church, I saw a sign listing all the times for its Masses. It was now about 8:45, and the English Mass began at 10 a.m. Vera had talked about hiking up a couple of mountains. I didn't feel I had time for that, so I decided to go into some of the shops and browse around now that they were starting to open up.

Displayed outside of every store were statues of Mary, Jesus, various saints, rosaries in all shapes and colors, books, jewelry, and a multitude of other religious gifts. I noticed there were publications that shared the actual messages Mary had given to the visionaries. I found a small paperback that contained every monthly apparition to the visionaries since they had begun in 1981. With the multitude of rosaries hanging from every possible place inside the store, and the hundreds I seemed to notice passing by other shops earlier, it seemed like a must-have souvenir. I looked around and settled on a simple one with wooden beads. As I walked out of the store with my book of messages, a few postcards, and rosary, I opened the bag. I looked at the rosary and laughed to myself. I didn't know how to pray the rosary.

It was about 9:45 when I noticed people streaming into the church. I realized I had better head over to get a seat. As I walked into the church, I noticed the elongated, colorful, stained glass windows. They let in so much natural light. The church had a simple beauty about it, and after having seen a bit of the town, I knew this was the focal point of Medjugorje. It seemed nobody could recall why such a large church was built for a small village back in the 1960s. Looking back, it seemed as if Mary had her hand in the construction knowing what future events would transpire there.

The church had a fairly modern design. In the back was the choir loft. The sanctuary was straight ahead with a raised altar. Off to the right was a large statue of Mary. By the time Mass began, the church was completely full. Being alone, I was able to manage some space in one of the pews about two thirds of the way back.

I looked behind me and noticed the choir loft. I thought to myself, "So there—there is where Mary appears!" It just seemed so simple. I would've thought that maybe they would have decorated the walls of the choir loft with gold leaf or something. But no, it was just a simple choir loft.

Mass began. By then, people were standing or sitting in the aisles. The entire church was just a sea of heads. The hymns began, and when some people started singing, everyone joined in. And not just in a half-mumble to themselves, but LOUDLY. I had never heard anything like it. I was sure people from a mile away could've heard the singing. These people were on fire, and it showed. Every response was practically a yell. Something here was truly moving them to be involved in the Mass in a way I had never seen before.

I'm not sure if it was the singing or what, but I left Saint James feeling energized. Usually I couldn't wait for Mass to end. I'd fulfill my obligation and want to move on with my day. But here I felt light on my feet. For some reason, even the kneelers didn't bother me, though they were basically a 4x4x36 rectangular piece of wood. But I didn't mind.

After Mass, I went outside and noticed lines of people waiting to go to confession. How unreal. I'd never seen more than two or three people in line at our church back home. Let's see, how long had it been since I'd last gone to confession? Well, it's not like I had killed anyone. "I don't think I need that right now," I told myself.

I decided to go to Apparition Hill, where Mary first appeared to the visionaries. Walking there, I passed a small field. Soon, many homes appeared to my left and right. It seemed like every third home was under construction, adding on a second story or an extension. The villagers knew there would be more crowds to come. Taxis passed by frequently, shuffling pilgrims back and forth. I noticed a group of people ahead of me. There was a large patio outside a house where people were crowding in from the street. As I walked up, I noticed that halfway up the cement stairs leading from the patio to the house was Vicka, one of the visionaries. In the book I had purchased, I couldn't help but look with wonder at the pictures of the visionaries in the early days when they were lined up in a row, all kneeling with eyes fixed upward, apparently in communication with the Virgin Mary. Now before my own eyes was Vicka. I had no idea they would be this accessible.

I had stumbled upon this visionary who delighted in sharing the messages of Mary to all who visited Medjugorje. Day in and day out, repeating the same thing over and over, she would never tire of speaking to the pilgrims and answering their questions. With my luck, this gathering was an English-speaking group, and Vicka spoke through a translator in her native Croatian.

Still a bit skeptical, I looked her over intently and listened carefully to what she said. She started out with a prayer. Everyone joined together in…"Our Father…Hail Mary…Glory Be…" On occasion she would smile, and the warmth that radiated from her was infectious. You just couldn't help but like her. Her explanation of how she saw Mary was very matter-of-fact. There was little emotion on her face, and her delivery was such that if you chose to believe what she said, great—if not, so be it. She wasn't saying she was special, above any of us, or that the world was in deep trouble. No, nothing like that. She understood her role perfectly. She was a messenger; she would be the medium, along with five others, to make known Mary's messages to the world.

Vicka said that when she has an apparition, there is at first a bright light, but one that does not blind. Then, Mary appears on a cloud. It is as if Vicka enters another dimension. The world around her disappears, and there is only Mary. She said Mary appears wearing a blue veil and gown. She sees her as a three-dimensional being, just as if she were seeing and talking with us, and that Mary's messages for us speak of the conversion of our hearts, fasting on Wednesdays and Fridays, praying, especially the rosary, attending Mass, and going to confession.

Vicka also mentioned that Mary had shown her and the other visionaries heaven, hell, and purgatory. She said that heaven really is indescribable. In heaven, the people are peaceful and at one with each other, and she could tell they love God so much. All smile and enjoy each other's company, and the love of God penetrates everywhere and everything. They all seem about the same age—in their thirties or so—and among them are angels with wings flying about. There is joyous music being played and sung, and a very warm light envelops them all. Vicka shared that Mary wants everyone to enter heaven to be with her and God, and though she cannot force people, she wants them to open their hearts to the Lord.

She said that we especially needed to pray for the souls in purgatory. That place is grey and blurry, and people inside are trying to get out. However, like an unbreakable cellophane wrap, she would see their arms and legs try to burst through this clear membrane, but not be able to puncture it. She said our prayers for their souls could help tremendously in releasing them into heaven.

She said that Mary then took them to hell—a huge lake of fire with smoke and flames stirring up from the surface. Into the turbulent lake are thrown those people who have refused God's love. They would then reappear looking nothing like their human form. The ones furthest from God are thrown deeper into the fire. They try in vain to get out, with their heads, arms, and legs thrashing about from the pain. They become black and take on the shape of grotesque creatures, some resembling animals. All the while they scream and yell, but no mercy ever comes their way. Vicka said she and the other visionaries were terrified and begged Mary to take them away back to their home. Mary did as they requested and mentioned that these were the people who turned their backs on God. They had chosen hell for themselves. God does not assign anyone to hell; it is of their own doing.

Vicka also spoke about how we need to pray for the youth, as they are growing up in difficult times. She said that the messages of Mary are real, nothing new or contrary to the Gospel, and that we need to take them to heart.

Vicka was asked if there were more people in heaven or hell. With a broad smile, she said there are many more people in heaven than in hell. She reiterated that the people in hell decided before they died that they wanted no part of God's kingdom.

When Vicka was through answering questions, she said that Mary would be appearing that same evening on the Hill of the Cross at 10 p.m. Wow! I was in luck! So I would get to see Mary after all! Why so late in the evening? And why up such a large mountain in the dark? Would there be lights up there to see her?

Well, whatever the case, I would definitely make a point to be there. It's not like I had any other plans.

Vicka then accepted petitions from people after a closing prayer. She said she would have the petitions placed before the Blessed Mother during her apparition in the church choir loft later that day. Vicka signed autographs without a hint of distaste as people flocked around her, pushing books, pictures, and postcards in her face to sign. I happened to have a postcard with me. Getting caught up in the moment, I edged toward her, and in due time I was standing right next to her, handing her my postcard. She signed it on the back, "Vicka." She had an unshakable humility about her and was so patient with the hordes of people clamoring for her attention. It was as if she knew that each person had traveled thousands of miles to be there, to see her, and to hear what Mary was saying. Because so many had come so far, she was more than happy to speak to them and sign her name for them. She was a person like anyone else, but now standing right before me, she was a person who received celestial visions on a daily basis, and that was a very cool thing to think about.

From Vicka's house, it was a short distance to the Apparition Hill trailhead. The Croatians call this Podbrdo Hill. The trail was made of reddish dirt with large white rocks smoothed over from the millions of people walking on them for the past eight years. There was no time for a single weed or blade of grass to grow on the trail from the continuous trampling. The exact site where Mary first appeared is about halfway up the mountain. The brush and plants give way to rock and dirt in a huge circular area. It was there that I found dozens and dozens of crosses of all sizes placed by pilgrims. Vera from the travel office had told me that a cross marked the spot where Mary first appeared, but she had forgotten to tell me there would be all these other crosses! So which one was it? Because it was early afternoon, there was no shortage of pilgrims. I asked a man where this cross was. He pointed out a large, unassuming cross, made of two metal planks that marked the spot.

I guess I expected something a bit more elaborate, but there it was. I went near it, sat down on a rock, and looked up at the cross and tried to imagine Mary floating above that spot about ten feet away from me. There is a more prominent statue of Mary now, but at the time there was just this simple cross. It was peaceful and quiet. The sun was out and it was quite hot, but the slight breeze was comforting. A blue ceiling tempered the bright sky while white, puffy clouds hung in the distance. I had been so set on looking for this cross on Apparition Hill that I almost forgot to take in the beautiful green landscape stretched beneath me. I saw a small, dirt road leading through fields to Saint James, where more homes circled around the church. Spaced around the village was a patchwork of farms and vineyards, which helped sustain the people of Medjugorje. Surrounding these small villages were mountains on either side, rising up sharply from the rural farmlands. In the distance to the west, I could see a trail switchback all the way up one side of the mountain I was facing. It was Mount Krizevac. My gaze followed it to the top, and upon it was a cross— *the* cross. It looked small from where I was sitting, but there on top of Mount Krizevac stood a huge concrete cross statue. This is where Mary was going to appear that evening, and I could feel the excitement welling up inside of me. I was literally hours away from seeing her!

Pondering from atop Apparition Hill, I glanced at the people around me. There were a few praying alone, but most were with family or friends. As I looked at the exact place where Mary had appeared to these six children, I wondered about the reality of the situation. I sat there looking around at the beautiful scenery and then back again at the cross on Apparition Hill.

After a while it dawned on me that I would have to make a choice—a choice that was very obvious and clear. What did I believe? Did I believe the Blessed Mother was coming here? Were the children speaking the truth? All the supposed miracles that seemed to take place here, could they be explained away? It was too early for me to answer, but sitting on that rock on Apparition Hill made me start to open up to what this place was about. There was a serenity that I began to feel.

I realized there was a distinct world that was set apart from our own: the spiritual realm. In Medjugorje, that world collided with the material and forced me either to accept what was happening with faith or to doubt any such existence. I wanted to believe, but like Saint Thomas and Saint Peter, I still had my doubts. I didn't understand that if these miracles were in fact taking place, why the Catholic Church didn't approve of them already? Why did they have to wait? Why did it take so long for this message to get to me, and only after having been in England?

Questions like these started to fill my mind. How does one come to terms with such a revelation? What if I don't want to believe? Would that make me a bad Catholic or Christian? I thought, "Why doesn't Jesus just come down and say a few words? Wouldn't that get people's attention? Why Mary? Why here? Why in a communist country?"

After an hour, I stood up. I looked at the metal cross and thought again, "Mary, the Mother of Jesus, chose that spot for some reason. And here I am. Somehow, in a crazy way, I managed to get myself here from Austria to this spot, to be near where the Blessed Mother has stood." What did it all mean to me? I felt like Charlie Brown in a baseball game. Charlie Brown wasn't really good at baseball—or any sport, for that matter—yet he found himself on the field anyway. He made himself present, and so was I. Maybe that was enough. There I was, in what was purportedly a very spiritual place. I didn't mind being there, but I just wondered what good it would do me in the end to have been here. I began to walk back down the hill.

As I was walked back down, I started to get hungry. Then I remembered. It was Friday, a fasting day. Vera, the young girl at the travel agency, said she fasts every Wednesday and Friday. "Oh no," I thought, "Could this be the beginning of denying self?" Part of me was saying, "Oh, just find a pizza place somewhere and take up the fasting some other time." Another part of me said to begin right then and there. I could have just shrugged off the request from Mary, but I thought, "No, this is my opportunity to embrace what could perhaps be a new beginning."

All throughout my travels in Europe, I tended toward the motto, "When in Rome..." I enjoyed taking part in the culture, food, and music that each town had to offer. That's what one does, right? And so I stuck to that in Medjugorje. If everyone else was fasting, certainly I could handle that too. Nobody wants to suffer alone. There was some comfort knowing that I could feel hungry and miserable along with everyone else. I felt since I was here, if I was truly to get the most of my experience, then I should commit to what was being requested here. After all, the villagers themselves apparently lived out the messages with great example. I was just planning on being here a couple of days, so surely I could fast a little.

I walked back to the house and went into my assigned room. I was the only one there among the several empty beds. Between Austria and arriving in Mostar, I had lived on honey and crackers. I sat on my bed and carefully spread the honey onto each cracker with my finger. I did it slowly, and knowing this was to be a "light" meal, I savored each bite and really took the time to appreciate the little snack. After eating several crackers, I laid down on the bed, picked up the small book I had found at the gift shop and read the messages Mary had given to the visionaries.

The small book included every monthly message from the Virgin Mary beginning in 1981 up until the past month, so the book was very current. The messages were simple in nature, and each one was like a short love letter to a son or daughter on how to live one's life. Really, it was nothing more than the messages given to us in the four Gospels: Turn to God and away from sin; love your neighbor; pray, fast, seek out reconciliation; attend Mass and convert our hearts to God.

Each message began, "Dear Children..." This is how Mary would address each of us: as a child of God. The messages were mixed with the tenderness and care a mother would provide to any child, and also with direct warnings for us to mend our ways and better our lives. Like any mother, she was letting us know she was right there for us in all our highs and lows. She wanted to guide us, comfort us, and more than anything bring us closer to her son, Jesus. For the next couple of hours, I read every message in that book and couldn't believe this was happening right in this town.

It was fascinating to think that the words I was reading came straight from Mary herself. The more I read, the more I started to believe that these words *were* from the Mother of God. The Blessed Mother would often reference the rosary. I grabbed the wooden rosary from the little bag I had purchased earlier and decided to break it in. I started out, "Hail Mary, full of grace, the Lord is with you, uh...ummm, Holy Mary, Mother of God, pray for us sinners now and at the hour of our death, amen." I tried saying it again, only the same thing happened. I had forgotten part of the prayer. This was ridiculous. I knew the prayer, didn't I? I had gone to Catholic school, for crying out loud. I remembered having said it in the past, but it had been a while. I kept going over that prayer again and again to no avail. I could not make out the first portion for the life of me—Google wasn't around yet, and I was too embarrassed to ask someone for help. Feeling pathetic, I gave up. Then my stomach began to rumble. I said to myself, "Suck it up, Dennis, just suck it up!"

Later that afternoon, I went to Saint James church and sat outside on a bench. Daylight would stay for several more hours. It was known that upstairs in the choir loft, the visionaries would gather there shortly after 6:30 p.m. and prepare for the apparition of Mary at 6:40. It had happened this way every night of the week without fail for years.

I was trying to prepare myself for what I was about to experience. There were quite a few people coming and going, milling around the church, sharing stories, laughing, praying with one another. Nobody seemed to notice me. For whatever reason, I had no interest in engaging anyone in conversation. I was content being by myself. People around me spoke so many different languages, and I wasn't always sure if they spoke English. It was kind of nice being anonymous. I found myself having short conversations with God. At the age of twenty-four, it certainly would not be unusual for me to be thinking about the future and what I was going to do with my life. Now I was looking at the world through the eyes of an adult.

As I was having one such talk with God, I noticed an American girl about the age of seven with her mom sitting across from me on another bench. Her mother pulled two rosaries out of her purse. She handed one to her daughter, and together they both began praying the rosary.

I had never in my life seen such a sight before—this beautiful little girl with her sandy blonde hair and tanned complexion looking so reverent while saying this prayer with her mother in her summer dress. I had never prayed with my mother outside of the meal blessing. It was very endearing to watch this mother and her daughter. They didn't know I was watching them, and people passed right by them without a second look. Praying in public was not a familiar sight where I grew up, but in Medjugorje, seeing two or more gathered in prayer was commonplace.

It occurred to me that if I listened closer, I could make out what they were saying and maybe figure out what part of the Hail Mary prayer I was missing. I tried not to look at them, even though their eyes were closed as they were saying the words aloud together. Then they said it: "Blessed are you among women, and blessed is the fruit of your womb, Jesus." That was it! Of course! How could I forget? Now that I knew, I repeated the words over and over again in my head. As the mother and daughter said the words of the rosary aloud with their eyes closed, I couldn't help but notice the calming effect they had on me. They seemed so at peace. Granted, it was in front of a church, but there was no awkwardness, nor shame. It seemed as natural as a mother reading her daughter a book, and it was such a beautiful a sight.

After a while, I got up, dried my sweaty eyes, and went to find a place inside the church so I could prepare myself for the apparition of Mary in the choir loft, which was soon to occur. As I headed into the church, I noticed the deep lines of people waiting to have their confessions heard by about a dozen or more priests. I thought, "Good for them." With twenty or more people in line, even if I wanted to go, the wait would probably be hours.

I couldn't recall the last time I had been to confession—probably years ago—but I wasn't going to wait.

The church was packed. I wished I had entered earlier to get a seat. I walked up the side aisle and noticed that, since the seats were all taken, people were sitting in the aisle. I found a spot near the front of the church and sat Indian-style. Nearby, an elderly, wrinkled Croatian woman with a head-scarf was sitting at the end of a pew. She had noticed a younger American man near her sitting in the aisle as I was. She got up from her seat, and though she didn't speak English, she motioned to the man to take her seat. The man's reaction was to say no, which he did, but the lady would not hear of it. She moved out of the pew and sat down where he had been sitting. He was very gracious, and I think I was as stunned as he was.

He was not an old man. He had not been complaining. What had made her want to do that? It was love, of course. After having received these messages from Mary, it was undeniable that this Croatian lady had taken them to heart and was truly living them out. I would later find out the entire town had been transformed by the apparitions and messages, and the villagers felt obligated to make all pilgrims feel welcome and comfortable. They were authentic examples of the love of God, living out God's love in all things, no matter how small, even giving up their own seat of comfort for the Croatian Mass, which was to begin following the apparition.

At 6:40, the apparition time had arrived. Surprisingly, most people in the church just went about praying. I realized they weren't looking up at the choir loft because the wall of the loft was too high to see a person's head, unless they were standing right at the edge. Every once in a while, someone would sneak a peek or take a picture, but there was really nothing there to see except the back wall. I thought, this was the big event? It all seemed so ordinary, other than the fact that the church was packed. There was a definite energy with all the people there, but it was subdued. The time of 6:40 came and went, and I wondered if maybe Mary wasn't coming this evening. After a few periodic glances to the choir loft, I didn't see her or anything else out of the ordinary. I wasn't sure if she had come or not, and I was too shy to ask anyone if I had missed something. Nobody else seemed to be as confused as I was. I had confidence in Vicka's earlier message that Mary would be appearing that evening at the top of Mount Krizevac at 10 p.m. I would be there for sure.

Mass began at 7 p.m. in the Croatian language. This was the Mass specifically for the residents of the village, though it was open to all. Many women wore veils over their heads and dressed modestly. While there were many other tourists amongst the congregation, it didn't matter who we were—we were there to celebrate the Mass together. Since it was in Croatian, I didn't understand much of what was said, but the cues were very familiar. That's the beautiful quality of the Mass—the format is the same wherever you are in the world. I found quite a bit of comfort in that. After Mass, I exited the church and found it still very light out, although the sun was about to set over the peaks of the mountains to the west of Medjugorje.

I looked up and saw the concrete cross upon the highest peak of Mount Krizevac, more than five thousand feet high. The cross was built in 1933 to commemorate the nineteen-hundredth anniversary of Christ's death. Prior to 1933, the villages in and around Medjugorje had experienced several years of drought. Farming was the lifeblood of the local community, much as it remains today, aside from catering to the pilgrims. The villagers came together, men and women, to carry the materials to build the huge cross with a prayer that Christ would recognize their strong devotion and faith and reward them with rain for their crops. Word has it there has not been a drought since.

Over the years, this cross became a lasting reminder not only of Christ's death on a cross for our salvation, but as a permanent reminder of the faith of those who live beneath it. The Stations of the Cross were also built along the path leading up to Mount Krizevac and served as part of the experience in climbing the mountain. As I stood outside Saint James, I noticed groups of people already making their way to the base of the mountain. It was now after 8 p.m., and I realized that if Mary was going to be at the top of that mountain in less than two hours, I should start making my way up.

As I left the church, I once again passed by lines of people waiting to have their confessions heard. There must've been at least eight priests sitting there, talking with people in the open air. I wasn't used to seeing confession take place outside a church. I thought I should get in line, but I didn't want to face what I knew, so I continued walking by. Dusk was settling in, and the sky looked brilliant as it shifted from a light blue above my head to a purplish night in the east. I walked along the road amid dozens of pilgrims. The crowd became thicker as I reached the base of the mountain. Once there, I began to ascend the mountain trail.

"Dear children! The cross was also in God's plan when you built it. These days, especially, go on the mountain and pray before the cross. I need your prayers. Thank you for having responded to my call."

Medjugorje Message, August 30, 1984

As darkness fell, I followed the trail of people up to the top of Mount Krizevac to see the apparition of the Mother of God. To most, the mountain is simply known as Cross Mountain. Thirty-six feet tall, the concrete cross stands like a sentry on the mountain, guarding the villages below. It was not an easy hike, especially in the dark. I used the light from other people's flashlights to get by. It was a rocky, steep climb. Groups of people sang songs and prayed on the way up. I recognized most of the songs, although they were sung in a different language.

It was an hour's climb to the top. Hundreds of people crowded around the huge cross. Some were praying, others singing. With the aid of other people's flashlights, I could see Ivan, one of the visionaries, praying near the base of the cross. The sky was pitch-black, but there were so many stars. Though that mountaintop was filled with people, the ambience was one of peace and love; there was no anxiety of being crammed. Since I was alone, it was easy for me to squeeze through the crowd and maneuver toward the massive cross.

After taking in my surroundings and catching my breath, I took a moment to reflect on what I was about to see. With flashlights from others filling the darkness, I looked at the silhouetted people around me as they sang songs of praise. They seemed to have no doubt about what was happening. They seemed confident in their faith, as if they were preparing for an event they knew for certain would occur. It was the same vibe I had felt in the church earlier. I felt slightly uncomfortable and didn't feel like I fit in.

At that point, I wasn't convinced of anything. I was impressed with the level of faith I was seeing around me, but I was alone and felt transparent. I knew no one there, and nobody knew me. How can one feel lonely surrounded by thousands of people? But I did. I was a bit envious these people had discovered something that was so foreign to me. They had such a joy in them. "How does one obtain that?" I asked myself. Excitement hung in the air, like a crowd waiting anxiously for fireworks to begin on the Fourth of July.

I had traveled almost four hundred miles from Austria to be at this place. Father John in Liverpool had taken my hand six weeks earlier and convinced me to come here. Looking back, there were so many ways it might not have happened. What if I hadn't been able to obtain a visa? What if I hadn't found that map of Yugoslavia or the lady who pointed out where to find Medjugorje? What if Mira wasn't at the train station when I arrived? Just where would I have ended up?

And now I found myself up on this mountain, where I was about to see the Mother of Christ. I did want to see Mary, but was I even worthy? Did I deserve to? Little did I realize I would be transformed from a curiosity-seeker to a seeker of faith.

At 9:58 p.m., cameras were put away and all singing and talking stopped. There was a hushed silence, except for the prayers of the visionaries as they spoke in Croatian. After a couple of minutes, their voices went silent, which meant they were conversing with Mary, but where was she? I scanned the sky, but I didn't see her. I glanced back at the visionaries, who were still looking up at the sky. I looked up again, yet I could see nothing but the multitude of stars and shadows of people from the dimmed flashlights and candles. Then I took a closer look at the people around me. Old, young, women, children, pilgrims, and Croatians alike weren't looking up. They were looking down. They were praying. Up until that time, I had been naïve, thinking that everyone who had climbed this mountain was going to see Mary. Why else would they climb up a mountain in the dark?

These people had faith in their hearts. They saw Mary in the depths of their souls, not up in the sky. At that very moment, I realized there was something more to this, something I had been missing. It dawned on me—I wasn't going to see her, and it was okay. Did I really need to see something to believe in it? Hadn't I always believed in God, yet never actually seen him? Something came over me, and a feeling of peace settled in my heart. I folded my hands, looked down, and prayed with the crowd in silence: "Mary, I don't really know why I'm here. Perhaps I was called to be here for some reason. If you are there and listening, I am here. Do with me as you wish and help me to live your messages."

When the apparition was over, Ivan spoke to the crowd through a translator about what he had seen. The translator said Mary had appeared with her arms extended over the crowd and that three angels had accompanied her. She prayed over the people gathered, and though she had no special message for us that night, she was joyful and happy and asked us to go in peace. In an instant, she flew away, leaving behind a lighted trail of a cross and went back to heaven, with the angels following her.

People began singing again, and some slowly began to descend the mountain. Then a miracle happened. All of a sudden, I was filled with an inexplicable joy and a warm sensation filled my entire body. My heart was racing as if I'd just had six cups of coffee. Simultaneously, I felt blissful and energetic. I know now that a belief took hold in me at that moment on that mountain that I hadn't expected. I was infused with the grace of conviction. I wasn't worthy, yet my short prayer was answered, and that grace convinced me it was all true. I thought I was going to physically see Mary, but now I didn't need that proof. I knew she was there in my midst, and that this was real. It had to be. I had been on the fence just minutes earlier, but now I was a believer.

If there hadn't been so many people in the way, I would've run down that mountain. To where, I had no idea, I just felt like running. I had never felt that way before. I had felt Mary's presence in a profound way and was now a different person because of it, different than when I had gone up the mountain. The spring in my step had me bouncing off the rocks on the way down like a skier on moguls, all without losing my breath. I made my way to the bottom of the mountain and walked past the church to the home where I was staying. I glanced back at Mount Krizevac, and amidst the blackness of the night was a continuous, thin, yellowish trail of light zigzagging from the top of the mountain all the way to its base. I stopped to take in the incredible sight of those multitudes of people still coming down from the mountain. I couldn't believe how quickly I had descended. When I got to the house, I laid down and tried to sleep. However, my mind was still racing, and my heart was pounding. I tossed and turned. I couldn't sleep for hours. Something was happening to me.

The next day, I awoke earlier than I wanted to, thanks to the roosters. I felt like I should have been out of it, but surprisingly I had a burst of energy that caused me to jump out of bed and prepare for the day. I went to the morning English Mass, and then spent a couple of hours reading and reflecting on the monthly messages from Mary to the visionaries. They were calling me to change my behavior. Later, I once again climbed Apparition Hill where Mary had first appeared to the children, and I found myself praying and contemplating things. I then had an epiphany. It occurred to me that if, in fact, I did believe Mary was appearing here, I must take her messages to heart. It was obvious the local townspeople of Medjugorje were living the messages and were great examples. They were so kind and generous to accommodate thousands of people invading their small town on any given day, having not only to cater to them, but also to *share* their Mother.

I felt as if God himself was giving me an ultimatum: either believe what was going on there or don't. After last night, did I dare not believe? I couldn't. It seemed too authentic to me, and that was where the internal battle began. Saying yes to Jesus and Mary meant more was going to be expected of me. I understood that, but I wasn't exactly looking forward to it. Giving in to Christ meant giving up selfish desires. We all have a selfish nature, and I'm certainly no different. It's kind of nice only having to worry about oneself. I would learn that this Christian road I was about to traverse meant more than going to church on Sunday. Like any relationship, it would require commitment. Ignorance would no longer be bliss; it was not going to be solely about me anymore.

I know I needed to work on my relationship with Mary's son, Jesus, and get to know him better. I also had to accept the Scriptures as the true word of God, and understand the relevance of the Holy Spirit and the Catholic Church. In the Bible, 2 Corinthians 5:17 says, "Whoever is in Christ is a new creation." That was the case with me. I realized that if I took these messages and apparitions to be true, then I must accept the entire package.

If I chose to be a Catholic, then Dennis, *be* a Catholic! Once I accepted that call, everything seemed to connect.

Too many Catholics I knew (myself included) were the "cafeteria" type—picking and choosing which aspects of the faith they wanted to believe in and adhere to, while *not* accepting other aspects they didn't agree with. It was time for me to decide. It was time for a lifestyle change.

I reflected on where I'd been with my life and what was ahead. In Medjugorje, Jesus, through Mary, touched me in a deep and personal way that I couldn't explain. Mary brought me closer to her son, Jesus. In Luke's gospel, Mary is referred to as the Magnificat. It made perfect sense to me. Mary's role in all of this is like that of a magnifying glass—as we look at her, we actually look through her, and her son, Jesus, becomes magnified. That is what she wants. What mother doesn't like to boast about her child? She wants to bring us closer to him.

I realize that many non-Catholic denominations don't see Mary this way, and it is truly unfortunate, as she *is* the mother of all, and her messages reach out to the world in just that way. The messages of Medjugorje are not urging everyone to convert to Catholicism, but rather to convert to Jesus. Mary makes herself available as an instrument through the Holy Spirit to communicate with us and guide us to Jesus.

I had spent much time in prayer when I was walking around the village of Medjugorje and the surroundings on the second day. There was at any given time an almost constant sea of people standing in line to attend the open-air confessional. Next to the priests were small signs stating which language they spoke: Italian,

German, French, Spanish, and so forth. It had been so long since I had been to confession—since I was a kid actually. I was reluctant to go, but deep down, I figured it wouldn't be such a bad thing. A part of me questioned the necessity of confessing to a priest at all.

As I walked past the confessional lines, throngs of people were always waiting. God knew my sins. I was sorry for them. That should be sufficient, I thought. Plus, I rationalized, "God, if you wanted me to go to confession, you would have put an English-speaking priest over there with a very short line." You see, I was still looking for faith on my terms, not God's. From a distance, I sat down to rest. Something inside was compelling me to go to confession. I wasn't sure what it was. I didn't want to go; I didn't need to go. Furthermore, I was not going to wait in a long line that was fifteen to twenty people deep.

Within seconds, I noticed a young priest casually walk by the long lines. He grabbed a chair and sat down. My heart started to beat a little faster. I continued to watch him as he set a sign out next to his stool. It said English. My heart began to beat really fast. But then I realized something. Coming from L.A., I knew crowd behavior. It was just a matter of seconds before people from other lines would rush over to him. I waited, and waited. Nobody moved. The priest just sat there. Then a force lifted me off my seat and pulled me in the direction of the priest. I never saw who did it, but I think it was the Holy Spirit. I was the first one to confess to the young priest.

He was from Brooklyn, and he made me feel very comfortable. I considered myself a decent person, but upon further inspection, I was without a doubt a sinner. The confession of my sins to that priest was a surprisingly great experience, and the grace I felt afterward—the grace of being forgiven—made me realize how powerful this sacrament is. It was humbling and healing.

I discovered why all those people would wait hours in line to confess their sins. It was the reason people went to Medjugorje in the first place. It was the reason they climbed Mount Krizevac. It was the crux of our belief. Jesus died for our sins. He died for us. He didn't have to, but he did. There is something special that awaits us in the next life, and he wants nothing to come between us, and that promised paradise. Sin is the only thing that can separate us, and we need that cross to remind us of that reality. One can look at the cross and consider many things, but what it should slap us with first and foremost is that we are sinners. When we gaze up at the crucifix and we see the suffering Jesus, we should think of our sinfulness. We put him there. He didn't deserve it—but he took it on for us. With this sacrament, we should be reminded that we do have a forgiving God, but we need the humility to go to him and seek that forgiveness.

Atop Mt. Krizevac, Medjugorje. My "mountain-top" experience.

We can't keep any secrets from Jesus. We can try to hide—as Adam and Eve did after they ate from the Forbidden Tree—but he already knows what we have done, and he is ready to forgive us. We just need to take that step and confess to a priest who is there in the place of Jesus.

Our secular society is doing a pretty good job of watering down sin to the point that almost anything can be justified. We can be fooled into thinking our sin is not so bad since "Everyone does it" or, "If it's legal, that must make it right." Sin is a reality for us. It needs to be talked about in addition to the forgiveness Christ offers. We need to be challenged. If we don't hear it from our pulpits, we certainly aren't going to hear about it on TV.

Toward the early evening of that second day, I was absolutely exhausted. I hadn't really done anything physical, but I was tired mentally. A combination of reading the messages from the previous eight years, praying, and being on this emotional high was sapping. I had pondered the truth of what I was seeing around me. Everyone was there in a group or with their families, so I had a unique perspective to take everything in without any need to engage others. At any given time, there were dozens of people in line for confession, as well as a constant stream of people going up and coming down from both Apparition Hill and Cross Mountain. The church was always overflowing with people for every Mass, regardless of the language. I wondered if it was possible that the people coming from all over the world were being duped. Was this one of the greatest shams ever? The testimony of six teenagers created all of this. Were they in it for financial gain? Did the Franciscan priests who oversaw Saint James Parish coordinate with the visionaries to bring economic prosperity to their small town?

I knew something inside my soul was different—and it felt good. If it was a sham, the Catholic Church would condemn it as such, and I would've submitted to that. However, if it got me going to Mass regularly, saying the rosary, praying, fasting, and appreciating my faith, then what could be so wrong with that? I went to bed early that evening knowing why I had come to this place. God did have a plan for me, and I just needed to follow it. A seed was planted, and I knew it would grow. I knew I had my work cut out for me in terms of re-educating myself about this Catholic faith I had grown up with.

I had told my Mostar family, the Vrbanec's, I would be back on the third day, so I planned on taking the bus back to Mostar the following day. As the bus drove away from the exact spot where I had been dropped off, I looked one last time out the back window where the dust was being kicked up. I glanced at Saint James and took in those twin steeples. I looked in the distance to where Mount Krizevac stood tall, and I silently recalled my mountain top experience two nights before.

Once back at the Mostar bus station, I was able to find my way to the Vrbanec family home. They greeted me, and more food came my way. Nela came over, and it was nice to have an English-speaking conversation with her. I gave her a brief summary of my short trip to Medjugorje, and she was very happy for me, adding that she could sense there was something a bit different about me from before. She patiently translated bits and pieces of my story for the Vrbanec's, and they nodded with approval.

Later in the afternoon, Nela and Tony gave me a walking tour of Mostar. We visited the World War II Memorial and walked across the famous Mostar Bridge. Nela pointed out places of interest along the way. There seemed to be quite a few mosques, and as she was Muslim, she gave me a brief history of that part of their country. Every now and then, there were soldiers standing guard at various places with guns. Nowadays this would not seem out of place, but twelve years before the 9/11 terrorist attacks in the U.S., it was definitely a scene I wasn't accustomed to anywhere else. I hadn't seen any armed soldiers in my travels in Western Europe.

The next morning I exchanged hugs and good-byes with the members of the Vrbanec family and Nela, and I made my way to the bus station. From Mostar, I boarded a bus that took me south through Croatia's beautiful Adriatic coast, where I would catch a ferry to Italy later that afternoon.

Once in Italy—Brindisi, to be exact—I was able to use my first-class Eurail pass for the trains, and how nice it was to get back to these familiar Western European trains! They were clean and smoke-free. The fact that I was no longer in a communist country brought a sense of relief that I would be safe from here on out. I would visit Rome, Venice, Bologna, Pisa, and then Greece, where I would spend several days in Athens with my cousin Liz and her husband, Terry, who worked as a doctor for the U.S. Embassy there. They had just had a baby girl, and it was great to see them. I visited some of the Greek isles, which included spending a couple of nights on the beach on Mykonos—literally on the beach, since all accommodations were full.

From Greece, I would travel to Spain, where I would spend four weeks living with a host family in Madrid. Before Matt and I had left for Europe, Matt had enrolled in an intensive Spanish class that began in September, giving us three months to travel. He suggested I join him. With him now in Japan, I decided to stick with my plans and go through with the class anyhow. Having just graduated a couple of months earlier, I wasn't that thrilled about going back to school, but I figured I would just go with it. I knew being in such an environment would help increase my very limited Spanish vocabulary.

I stayed with a family in Madrid, along with two other students, an American and a German, both about my age. My American roommate and I traveled one weekend to Barcelona and another to Portugal. Sadly, I was not too familiar with the story of Fatima, so I never made a trip to that Portuguese village where the Blessed Mother had appeared to three young visionaries named Jacinta, Francisco, and Lucy back in 1917.

I attempted to share with those I met in Spain about Medjugorje and was still surprised people had not heard of the events transpiring there. I fasted at least once a week and prayed the rosary daily. Sitting in a class for twenty-five hours a week didn't diminish the fire in my soul. I just knew the conversion experience was not going to be a fleeting moment, but would remain with me for a long time.

After four weeks, my time was up with my host family. I had taken in many of the sights of Madrid but was ready to head home. I still had two nights before flying out. Due to the high demand, I stayed at two different hostels near the airport. What was interesting was that at each hostel I had a roommate. Both roommates were boys my age who happened to be from Santiago, Chile. They didn't know each other, and with all the guys I had shared rooms with over the past four months, I couldn't recall any who had been from South America, much less Chile. Now on my last two days in Europe I had met two from the same city. I knew a girl back home whose family was from Chile—Hedy. The girl who forgot to tell me her phone number had changed. I wondered what had ever happened to her.

My flight from Madrid to L.A. was uneventful, but I was still very much on a spiritual high. When I got back home, it was bittersweet. Dad, always a model of health, was in the hospital. I had to go see him straight from the airport.

Chapter 4

THE WORD

*"Dear children! Today I call you to the renewal of prayer
in your homes. The work in the fields is over. Now devote
yourselves to prayer. Let prayer take the first place in your
families. Thank you for having responded to my call."*

Medjugorje Message, November 1, 1984

I couldn't recall Dad ever being in the hospital before, so I was
concerned. He had been having a lot of pain around his abdomen.
Doctors had been running tests for a couple of days, but they
couldn't seem to find what was wrong. When I arrived at the
hospital, my family was all there, and when I said "Hola," they all
laughed and answered, "Hola!" For the previous four weeks, that
greeting had become second nature for me. I wasn't trying to be

funny, especially with all of us around Dad's bedside, and I still had no idea why he was there. I had just experienced the most incredible four months of my life, and it was topped off with a deeper level of spirituality.

Since my family had been there a while, they left me alone to spend some time with Dad. After using the restroom, Dad walked slowly to get back into bed. I could see he was experiencing extreme pain. I felt totally helpless, as there was nothing I could do for him. While he got settled into bed, I tried to make sure he was as comfortable as he could be under the circumstances. He then looked me in the eye and said, "So, Dennis, tell me about this place called Medjugorje." I could tell he was still feeling pain so I didn't want to spend hours explaining everything to him. He had received my over-the-top postcards telling him that we needed to pray together when I got home. Of the many postcards I had sent, he knew my belief in Medjugorje was like no other. I just explained the simple messages that Mary was giving to us all and how Medjugorje was just a truly special place and that he and Mom should try to go someday. Never one to reveal much about his feelings, much less his spiritual nature, I figured it would fall on deaf ears, but I thought maybe, just maybe, that could come true.

It turned out Dad had gallstones, and he needed to have his gall bladder removed. In the end, we weren't sure why it took so long to diagnose the problem. Once everything was removed, he was back to normal. It was a bit of a scare at first, but we were all relieved when Dad was released to go home a couple of days later.

I spent the next few days and weeks filling my parents and my family in on my travels and everything I could about Medjugorje. My grandmother was visiting us from Chicago then, as she did every year. I told her all about my trip and the messages from Mary.

Within a couple of days, she said she wanted to go to confession after more than twenty years! She went, as did my parents, who admitted it had been some time since they had been, too.

Shortly thereafter, our parish priest friend, Father Ferraro, came by our house for a visit. It was the first time I had seen him since I had come back from my trip. I was so thrilled to tell him what I had experienced. Finally, I had found someone whom I wouldn't have to explain all of Medjugorje to. Being a priest, he would know all about it, and perhaps even have been there himself. Or so I thought.

When I told him I had been there, he said to me, "Dennis, you don't really believe all that stuff, do you?" I was taken aback and speechless. He was the last person I had expected to be critical of such events. I came to find out later that it wasn't that he didn't believe in Medjugorje or Marian apparitions, but just that he didn't place a lot of significance in them.

Over time I would discover that there were many clergy as well as lay people who either didn't believe in the events of Medjugorje, or like Father Ferraro, didn't need them to enhance their faith life. It didn't make them any less Christian, of course, but it became a lesson for me that everyone has his or her own style of faith and belief. The fact that the Church hasn't approved the apparitions in Medjugorje also gives them a right to abstain from accepting them. *That* they believed in the major tenets of faith was important. *How* they believed in those tenets was not for me to judge. The church doesn't obligate the faithful to believe in Marian apparitions, so that was to be respected. Not everyone saw or felt what I had. What I had received was a gift.

I hadn't been home more than a month when I learned that the one, the only, Paul McCartney would be playing a concert in L.A. at the Forum Arena. I felt God was blessing me with this Beatles legend for having gone to Medjugorje. The Liverpool connection was just too coincidental. That November, I took in one of the greatest live performances of my life. Of course for many, the voice or the quality of the music wouldn't have mattered. Though all of that was spectacular, just being in the same venue with Paul was worth the price of admission. It had been thirteen years since he had toured, and for the first time Paul felt comfortable playing a collection of Beatles songs—some of which the Beatles themselves had never performed live because they had stopped touring in 1966. In fact, half of the songs Paul performed on any evening were from the Beatles, and the other half were from his solo efforts and his hits with the band Wings.

When Paul sang "Yesterday" and "Let It Be," women all around me were sobbing as if they were at a funeral. The show was moving and exhilarating, and Paul looked like he was having the time of his life. Just like his recordings, his voice sounded almost angelic at times, yet it still had the power to kick in such rock classics as "Birthday" and "Sgt. Pepper's Lonely Hearts Club Band."

When I was growing up, music took much more precedence than textbooks or novels. Since my return from Medjugorje, the Holy Spirit had put a desire in me to learn more about my faith through reading. This thirst became unquenchable as I found myself reading book after book about various saints, the Catholic Church, the Bible, and other spiritual topics. Of course, the Bible struck me the most. I enjoyed reading the New Testament, which included Paul's letters, the Gospels, and the Acts of the Apostles. I had heard most of it before, but for the first time, the readings actually meant something to me and came alive. I could relate them to my life, and the words were now having a positive impact on me. This was no longer fiction—the words were challenging, yet their inherent truth led me to view the world as Jesus wanted me to see it, through eyes of faith.

Four months earlier, I would have had no interest in reading anything spiritual or religious. I believed in God and I respected the beliefs of others, but that was about it. The more I learned, the more I realized what I didn't know. As I read the Bible more and more, I realized it was a guidebook to heaven, which the messages of Medjugorje only reinforced. I was reminded of the great story we have in Jesus, his mother Mary, and the salvation he obtained for us.

There were a couple of bookstores near my house that had the spiritual reading I was looking for. One was a Christian bookstore, another Catholic. I became a regular at both, digging into all kinds of books. I discovered the Daughters of Saint Paul Bookstore in West L.A., which had an even larger selection of books and gifts. I then came across reprints of several articles that appeared in a Myrtle Beach, South Carolina, newspaper. The author, Wayne Weible, had been a frequent visitor to Medjugorje and had received an inner locution (a private revelation) from the Blessed Mother, and felt compelled to share her messages and the story of Medjugorje. His articles were surprisingly objective to me, and the fact that he was writing this as a practicing Lutheran in a secular newspaper made it even more interesting. Shortly thereafter, I picked up his new book, *Medjugorje: The Message*, which spoke about his conversion experience in Medjugorje in an exciting way and became a best-seller. In my opinion, it continues to be one of the best introductory books about Medjugorje. Having read this after my first trip made me long to go back again in May 1990.

I re-read the monthly messages from Medjugorje. I wanted to live those messages the best I could. Fasting was a message that simply could not be ignored. I began fasting on Wednesdays and Fridays, which made me appreciate food in a whole new way. Sometimes I would not eat anything until after 3 p.m. on those days. Other times, I would have a piece of toast for breakfast and maybe a yogurt or an apple for lunch. Then, without any snacks, I would have my main meal at dinner. Over the years, I have lost some discipline, and my fasting regretfully comes and goes. I do fast, but it's not always centered on food.

One can fast from the simple pleasures of life. Maybe it's not listening to music or talk radio for a day while commuting to and from work. Instead of indulging in those pleasures, say the rosary or spend time in prayer. Sometimes I'll go without dessert or a cocktail when I really feel like one. I don't think Mary is asking us to starve ourselves, but rather for us to simply instill a little discipline in our lives. Doing this serves two purposes: one, offering self-sacrifice up as a prayer for various intentions; and two, making us appreciate what we do have a little bit more.

Saint Lawrence parish had a daily Mass at noon. I started to attend Mass every day as part of my attempt to make prayer a daily part of my routine. Though I could never imagine myself sitting down with Mom and Dad and actually praying, I thought I'd give it a try. Mom, a bit more open-minded to it at first, actually taught me the fifteen mysteries of the rosary. Up until then, I had thought one was supposed to just contemplate on the words of the Our Father and Hail Mary while praying. It had never occurred to me that the rosary was actually the story of our redemption, beginning with the Angel Gabriel appearing to Mary and announcing her pregnancy with the Son of God, all the way through to the passion and death of Jesus on the cross, and then to his resurrection. Since then, Pope John Paul II has added five more Luminous Mysteries, which complete the life of Jesus between his presentation in the temple and his ministry in adult life.

When I heard Vicka state that the Blessed Mother wanted us to pray as a family and to pray the rosary together, I thought, "How nice, but not in a million years in my family." We were all Catholic, of course, but my parents were not brought up that way and were not comfortable vocalizing prayers. It had nothing to do with their spirituality or belief; it was just a matter of helping them get over their discomfort of praying out loud. I simply asked them to join me whenever I was going to pray. In time, Mom was praying with me. Within a few days, so was Dad. To me, that was a miracle.

One day, shortly after Mom and I had started praying the rosary together, there was a knock at my door. It was Bob, an old acquaintance from school. We weren't the closest of friends, but through mutual friends like Matt, we would hang out from time to time. I can't even remember why he came over, but I told him that my mom and I had just started to pray the rosary and that he was welcome to join us. I thought he'd make a quick exit, but to my surprise, he said okay. So I grabbed an extra rosary and the three of us sat there and prayed together. My plan was to go to the noon Mass at Saint Lawrence afterward, and again to my surprise, Bob said he would join me.

What was interesting was that the monsignor who said the Mass that day was a retired Irish priest who filled in during the weekday Masses. He had been the amiable, yet put-you-to-sleep pastor of the church when I was a kid growing up, just before

Father Ferraro came along. Rest his soul, he wasn't the most animated priest. He had a very monotonous voice, and while he was nice, he always seemed disconnected from the congregation and detached emotionally. Though he may have had some uplifting things to say when I was younger, I remember him only as being a kind, but boring priest. It had been years since I had seen the monsignor, and now here I was with him during Mass. His homily was short and to the point, making several references to how we can gain the kingdom of heaven based on one of the readings.

With Bob at my side, the monsignor, as if he knew what was in our hearts, said, "The rosary is something that is not prayed as often as it used to be. It's a beautiful prayer. It will bring us closer to Jesus, and it's unfortunate more people don't take advantage of it. People are curious as to what they need to do in order to get to heaven. I'm pretty certain that if you pray the rosary every day, you will go to heaven."

Bob and I took one look at each other. We didn't need to say a word—the expressions on our faces said it all. I almost jumped out of my seat because rarely had I heard any priest mention the rosary in his homily. And to have heard it right after praying the rosary with Bob for the first time was a strange coincidence.

"If you pray the rosary every day, you will go to heaven."

Was he right? Was it really that simple? Before Medjugorje, if I had heard that, I may have started praying the rosary every day in the same way you go to work each day to earn a paycheck. With an enlightened sense of faith now, I realized that it wasn't because of praying the rosary that one would get to heaven. Praying the rosary is a byproduct of the faith of an individual who has already dedicated his or her life to Jesus and trusts in his guidance and providence. The rosary is one of many tools that connect us with Jesus and his mother in a more intimate way. There are powerful promises Mary herself has passed down through the ages for those who pray the rosary, including her special protection against Satan, being released from purgatory, and not dying without receiving the sacraments. It is encouraging to see that even non-Catholics are praying the rosary and benefitting from its graces. It is meant for all to pray, not just Catholics.

I came to enjoy praying the rosary with Mom and Dad at home. I felt so bonded to them, more than ever before. To this day, I don't know if Dad was doing it out of love for me because he knew how much I wanted us to pray as a family, or because he really wanted to do it on his own. For months this went on, sharing the peace of prayer with Mom and Dad.

It wasn't long before they shared some news with me they were very excited about. Soon they would be leaving on a journey of their own to Medjugorje. My parents decided they would go the following year. I never thought they would take such a trip. I happily checked that off my answered prayer list.

I was also excited to hear there would be an inaugural Marian Conference coming up in Irvine. This allowed thousands of people to gather for a weekend of prayer, fellowship, and the sacraments in a large venue with guest speakers involved in Medjugorje. I was pleasantly surprised that some family friends and my godparents, with some of their children whom I had grown up with, were willing to take part in the conference. Other family friends joined in as well.

In the months after my return from Europe, I would run into family members and friends, and the conversation would quickly turn to my trip to Europe. It wouldn't be long before I would start rambling on about my experience in Medjugorje. That, in turn, would lead to more questions, and next thing I knew I was becoming a witness for the messages from Medjugorje. As word got around, I was asked to speak at a couple of parishes and explain the events transpiring there. As much as I had been in the dark about the apparitions, it seemed that just as many others were as well. In the same way the priest from Liverpool, Father John, had taken his time to tell Matt and I what was going on, I also felt obligated to share my experiences with others and encourage them to go there if they could.

In May 1990, my parents, along with my uncle Vic and aunt Dolores from Illinois, made the trip to Bosnia-Hercegovina and stayed with the Vrbanec family in Mostar. Another answered prayer. They spent most of a week in Medjugorje and the highlight of their trip was experiencing the miracle of the sun and having Vicka pray over each of them.

As I was helping Mom and Dad with the logistics of their trip, I couldn't help but catch the fever of wanting to be back at that special place and stay longer than a couple of days this time. I had subscribed to every newsletter I could find about Medjugorje, including a new *Medjugorje* magazine. There was even a phone number to call on the twenty-sixth of each month for the latest monthly message from Our Lady (given on the twenty-fifth). I was anxious to find out the latest news and see how the visionaries' lives were changing. A lot was happening over there, but I wondered if I was changing to the extent God was calling me to.

Chapter 5

Your mother should know

"Dear children! In your life you have all experienced light and darkness. God grants to every person to recognize good and evil. I am calling you to the light which you should carry to all the people who are in darkness. People who are in darkness daily come into your homes. Dear children, give them the light! Thank you for having responded to my call."

Medjugorje Message, March 14, 1985

While I was doing my part in praying and converting, I longed to return to Medjugorje, the source of my newfound spirituality. The Bosnian war was still a couple of years off, and at the time, there was nothing in the air suggesting turmoil in that region. I mentioned my intentions to my sister and brother-in-law, Dave, who lived a few hours away in Ridgecrest in the high desert. Dave said he wanted to join me.

My only sister, Julie, is four years older than I. Shortly after her high school graduation, she moved down to San Diego with two girlfriends. It wasn't long before she met Dave, a sometimes-employed carpenter who liked drinking and drugs.

I remember my parents talking to each other about this new boyfriend of Julie's. Like any parents protective of their only daughter, they wanted the best for her. Dave was not the knight in shining armor they had been hoping for. Julie had a couple of boyfriends in previous years, none of whom managed to make a good impression. Their negative influence would cause her to stay out way beyond her curfew, and when she got grounded, she still snuck out to meet them. My parents were sad to think that she would never find someone good enough for her. Her rebelliousness took a toll on them, and my parents' relationship with my sister became very strained.

Dave had not held a steady job for a long time, which concerned my parents. He was a handsome guy with a muscular build, but he had an angry side and a bad temper. He had the ability to intimidate and did so when he saw fit.

So now he and my sister were in love. Wonderful! Looking back, I don't know if my sister had grown up a bit or if the advice my parents were giving her was finally making sense—or a combination of the two—but she finally realized after a year or so that she didn't want to be a part of that lifestyle. Julie gave Dave an ultimatum: if she was going to stay with him, he had to give up the drugs. It was what Dave had known for years, and to give it up would be difficult. Dave grew up with two very abusive and alcoholic stepfathers at whose hands he suffered years of physical and emotional abuse. It was no surprise his behavior was a reflection of this dysfunctional upbringing.

Though Dave said he would abandon drugs, he often went back to the same routine. Julie knew Dave needed to be out of that environment and away from his negative friends, and in time, Dave concluded it was time to settle down. He found a good-paying job far away from San Diego in the California high desert. They moved to Ridgecrest shortly thereafter, where he began steady work and weaned himself off of drugs and eventually, alcohol.

After Julie saw such positive change in Dave, they were married, and within a couple of years, Dave had an interest in joining the Catholic Church. He had gone through the RCIA program and chosen me to be his sponsor. My older brothers had moved away after high school, so they didn't get to know Dave in quite the same way I did. I don't think he knew many other Catholics, and though I was happy to sponsor him, I felt like a hypocrite. I was partying it up at spring break in Palm Springs the day before he was confirmed in the Church. Some example I was. This was a few years before my going to Medjugorje, so I still had some growing up to do myself.

I would often drive the three hours to Ridgecrest just to hang out with Julie and Dave for the weekend. I came to learn a lot about my new brother-in-law. It made me proud to see how well he treated my sister and the huge steps he had made in providing for them, as well as being so loving to the rest of our family. In the end, I believe the lack of dysfunction in our family was what Dave longed for, and over time he embraced our family as much as we embraced him. His love for Catholicism and the Mass was inspiring. He even formed a lunchtime Bible-sharing group with some of his coworkers. Dave was on fire for the Lord and excited to have the opportunity to go to Medjugorje. I was looking forward to sharing it with him.

After five years of marriage, my sister wasn't sure why she wasn't becoming pregnant. After some doctor visits, the news was not good: she was unable to conceive. Fortunately, a couple of years later, they were blessed to adopt a boy from birth, Jason. A beautiful boy in every way, Jason brought an immense joy to Julie and Dave, and they were grateful to finally have a child after so many years together.

In May 1990, Dave joined me for my second visit to Medjugorje. This time, I was more prepared; through a series of long-distance calls, I was able to connect with the Vrbanec family again, along with another family in Medjugorje who were happy to have us stay with them during our visit. Julie asked us to pray in Medjugorje for the opportunity to adopt another child so Jason could have a sibling.

So with that intention, Dave and I flew off for a week in Medjugorje. Dave was not much of a world traveler, in part because he didn't like flying. His zeal for the Lord was so strong, however, that he overcame his fear. After a short layover in London, we flew to Dubrovnik, where we visited the Old City. From there, we boarded a bus that wound alongside the turquoise blue waters of the Adriatic coast of Croatia and then inland to Mostar. We met with the Vrbanec family and Nela, who were happy to see me again and meet Dave.

It was great seeing them, and we got caught up with the events in our lives. The following day, Dave and I were on the bus to Medjugorje. Less than a year had passed, but already I could see the changes to the small village once we arrived. More than before, signs of renovations and additions were everywhere. It seemed like every other home was under construction, adding on another bedroom or a second story in order to accommodate pilgrims. We stayed with a family that spoke little English, but they were very hospitable. They had an older son, Marko, who was in his mid-thirties. He spoke broken English, and almost looked like Jesus himself, with piercing eyes, darkly tanned skin and long, wavy brown hair. There were several other guests staying in other rooms in the same house. We came together at breakfast and dinner, and shared stories and got to know each other during our week there.

Being mid-May, it was much cooler than my previous August trip, and the surrounding mountains were now colored in green. Dave and I took in all of the popular sights of Medjugorje and the neighboring villages, visiting Apparition Hill and Cross Mountain, attending Mass at Saint James, and praying the rosary daily. At the end of our first English Mass, Dave felt the Holy Spirit enter his soul in a very profound way. He had a strange sensation come over his body that he had never felt before, but it was very positive. I thought it could be a health issue, but he assured me it was all very spiritual. The Spirit started to open his soul to the graces he would receive while there.

One morning, after having been inspired by Wayne Weible's account of hiking Cross Mountain before daybreak, we found it in ourselves to wake up at 4 a.m. and hike up that holy mountain in the dark, praying at each of the Stations of the Cross on the way. Once we reached the top of the mountain, we thought we would be the only ones who would venture out so early. Apparently others had read Wayne Weible's book, too. There were dozens of people up there before the sun's rays had even begun to penetrate the sky. Some had even spent the night up there in sleeping bags.

Despite that, there was a quiet reverence present, as if we were in a cathedral. After all, this was where I had that tremendous experience the year before, when Mary entered my soul during an apparition. Though it was a bit chilly at that early hour, we were warm from the hike up. We read scripture together and watched the sun rise over the eastern mountains. After praying together, we separated for about a half-hour, and each spent some one-on-one time with God. I gazed at the villages below and once again at the steeples of Saint James Church.

Now that I had read so much about the history of the apparitions, I could visualize the children walking from their respective villages to the church where Father Jozo, the original parish priest, had protected them from the police in those early days. Those were extremely tense times, but despite Father Jozo being imprisoned and tortured for eighteen months, the apparitions continued every single day. Early on, Father Jozo was a skeptic, and it wasn't until he was praying in the church that he heard a voice say to him, "Protect the children." At that very moment, the children tore into the church in tears, trying to escape the police looking for them. Father Jozo hid them that day, yet it didn't stop the government from setting up police blockades around the clock and detaining and questioning pilgrims. In order to control the media, they imprisoned the only two journalists who were favorable towards the apparitions. The children's parents were also taken into custody and ordered to forbid their children from going to the church. Because the apparitions continued, albeit at secret locations early on to evade the communist authorities, Father Jozo was held responsible and sentenced to prison.

On the way back down the mountain, we visited the site of the Blue Cross at the base of Mount Podbrdo, where the Blessed Mother appeared to the visionaries when the police were staking out Apparition Hill in the early days. The Blessed Mother sometimes still appeared to one or more of the visionaries at this location. As we walked around, we stumbled upon the visionary, Ivan, in front of his house speaking with a few other pilgrims. We invited ourselves into the conversation, and through an interpreter, we were able to hear his thoughts in a very casual setting on how the messages from the Blessed Mother were meant to put us into action and to better ourselves.

Dave and I in the wine cellar of our Medjugorje hosts.

After my first trip to Medjugorje, I learned of all the apparent miracles that accompanied the apparitions. It is said that the Croatian word for peace, *mir*, was spelled out in the sky above Medjugorje in a cloud. Many would experience the miracle of the sun, where they could literally stare at the sun for minutes at a time without any harm to their eyes. Some would see the sun spinning in circles, casting colorful rays of light outward, while the inner circle of the sun appeared as the host. Others would say the sun "danced" around the sky, bobbing up and down and going from side to side. This was similar to the miracle that roughly seventy thousand experienced and testified to in Fatima, Portugal, in 1917, when Mary last appeared to the three visionary children there.

There are documented cases of blind people who gained their sight in Medjugorje, along with others who had serious medical conditions and were miraculously cured upon their visit. The numbers are too great to count of those who suffered various addictions, depression, estrangement from family members, or other life challenges and overcame those challenges through their visit to Medjugorje and found forgiveness and love. I'm confident the numbers are even greater for those who were lukewarm in their faith or perhaps absent from it entirely, but who recommitted themselves to God, back to the Church, and back to being a faithful servant of Jesus.

One night at dinner, our host, Marko, was speaking to Dave and me in his broken English about some of the unusual things he'd seen in Medjugorje. It was very frustrating because we could only make out a few words in every sentence, so it was difficult to grasp what he was saying. We missed many of the details, but there was a time he saw a butterfly that he considered a miracle from the Blessed Mother to him. We couldn't make out when or where this happened, but the expression he had on his face while telling us this story made it quite believable.

A couple of hours later, Dave, Marko, and I found ourselves going up to Apparition Hill for a 10 p.m. apparition to the visionaries. We followed Marko's lead. He led us off the usual path and went up the hill through thick thistle bushes, and we were amazed at how quickly we made it up the hill. As we got closer to Ivan, we meandered through the crowd, bouncing from rock to rock, making our way higher. We were surprised we had made it through Marko's shortcut without getting a single scratch.

We were about twenty-five yards from the visionary Ivan. As before, when I witnessed the apparition on Cross Mountain the previous summer, there was a solemn anticipation in the crowd as they sang hymns and prayed in preparation for the apparition. It was standing room only. Some had found large boulders to sit on, but for the most part, people were standing, and many appeared to be in a very prayerful state.

The night was cool and dark, and like a Christmas tree lit up by lights, so was the hillside by those carrying flashlights. I'd never been to a Grateful Dead concert before, but friends of mine who had would often comment on the "vibe" at their concerts. Call it "brotherly love" or "peace and harmony," but this hippie kind of love seemed to be quite present among the pilgrims making their way up the hill. You felt that each person there, was a close family member, who would give the shirt off their back if you asked for it.

Like so many times before, Ivan's voice went silent once Mary appeared to him. It became very quiet as he conversed silently with Mary while his gaze was fixed at the starry sky above. After a few minutes, his eyes closed and he looked down as if to pray and give thanks. The apparition had ended, and the interpreter began translating the message from Our Lady that evening. Ivan told us that Mary had asked us to continue to convert our hearts, and that God could do so much more for us if we opened our hearts. Ivan also said that Mary was happy that we were there, and she would impart her blessing upon us all that evening.

Unlike before, there was no supernatural feeling that came over me, or Dave. Of course I knew now that only the visionaries actually saw the Blessed Mother. I was looking up to the sky, if only to absorb the real sense that Mary had been right there in our midst. Then, before we could head down the trail again, something appeared in the sky out of nowhere. About thirty feet above our heads was a small light, almost as if it was a glow-in-the-dark hummingbird. It was a bright yellowish light, but it was very jittery, so it was hard to make out the exact form. Like a hummingbird, this "thing" hovered over us and wavered from side to side. It was blurry, and as each of us was trying to make out what it could be, it darted about twenty yards horizontally over to the left of the crowd. Gasps emerged from those assembled. Some people began to kneel. Just as it would seem to be still enough for us to see what it was, it would dart again to the other side of the crowd with lightning speed. Then it would do so again in a different direction. It did this for about a minute before disappearing before our eyes. Dave and I looked at each other and said, "What was *that*?"

A hummingbird was the only thing I can imagine that could move that fast and come to a complete stop and remain stationary in the sky. However, to my knowledge, there were no hummingbirds in Croatia that glowed in the dark. The light was definitely coming from a source within the object, and there was no way someone could have accurately kept their flashlight on this object with the random way it zigzagged above our heads. Dave and I could not help but think about Marko's butterfly story told to us earlier that evening. To this day, we have no idea what the light was, but everyone up on that hill that night was witness to it, and they were amazed.

During the week we were there, there were two days we emerged from the Croatian Mass to see people outside looking toward the sun. Dave and I both experienced that ability to look directly at the sun without any harm or discomfort. It was like looking at the moon, and I kept wondering how it was possible that my eyes could remain fixed on this sun, which at any other time would have burned my retinas to a crisp. At that time of the year, the sun was still fairly high in the sky, even in early evening. As I watched the sun, I could see it pulsate, and the brightness would darken and then brighten as if someone was adjusting a switch. I had not witnessed this before in my life and haven't since. We knew this was another grace bestowed on us and gave thanks to God for demonstrating once again that he was right there in our midst.

My second trip to Medjugorje was definitely more of a prayerful pilgrimage. It was an enriching time to spend with my brother-in-law, and it allowed me time to spend the day in prayer. I wasn't there to discover anything new, nor did I need to question the events taking place there. I was there simply as a pilgrim who believed. It was an affirmation of my need to continue my spiritual journey.

Near St. James Church, Medjugorje.

Though Dave and I experienced some amazing miracles on my second trip, the greatest of them occurred when we returned. While we were in Medjugorje, my sister Julie had received a phone call. My oldest brother Dave had a fiancé whose mother knew someone with a teenage daughter wanting to give up her child for adoption. When they told the pregnant teen's mother they knew someone who was looking to adopt, they didn't hesitate. God had answered our prayer, and my sister and brother-in-law soon found themselves with a newborn boy who we call our Medjugorje miracle baby. Twenty-two years later, my nephew Matt is doing well; he is a proud member of the U.S. Air Force and now married.

The summer of 1990 brought many changes for me. My parents had just retired. They were both fifty-five years of age, and by that time Dad had put in twenty-eight years at the same company. For years my parents had planned for this. They wanted to travel and volunteer before they were too tired or frail to take on such adventures. So with careful planning and saving, my parents retired, joined the Peace Corps, and after that, the Red Cross.

Normally it was not easy for the Peace Corps to assign married couples to a location, especially ones who were older. Most people assume the volunteers are fresh out of college, excited to see the remote regions of the world and help others. That stereotype is certainly there, and you don't find many senior citizens joining the ranks of young twenty-somethings. However, that was what I always appreciated about my parents. Their youthful approach to life and zeal to experience everything were evident to all they came in touch with.

Fortunately, with my parents both having a business and management background, the Peace Corps sent them off together to the Fiji Islands. For the next three years, they helped the Fijians with their businesses, including a lumber mill, coconut processing plant, and sugar mill. They were assigned to the Lau group, a cluster of small islands east of the two main islands where most of the Fijian population resides. They would hop on a boat and sometimes a small plane, traveling from island to island to give workshops on various business concepts and time management to people in the small villages.

The agreement was for me to stay at the house, pay rent and maintain it. I was now a college graduate living at home with a tremendous zeal for the Lord. I was managing the sales office and was responsible for recruiting and training the sales force which generally consisted of college students. I asked myself if overseeing door-to-door salesmen was what I wanted to continue to do. I had been going door-to-door throughout the greater L.A. area for over five years. I could write a separate book just about those experiences. The money had been good all along and the schedule very flexible, but now armed with a degree, I felt I should pursue something with more of a future. In June of that year, I felt it was time for a change.

I searched the job openings in the papers, but nothing appealed to me. I prayed about it and continued to attend daily Mass. One day, in one of the pews was an old school buddy named Larry. I hadn't seen him in years. We had attended Saint Lawrence Elementary together. He was a funny kid. He loved to joke around and poke fun, though that poking often led to other classmates poking right back and chasing after him. Larry loved to be chased. Every so often during recess, you could see him running ahead of one, two, three or more boys across the grass field with a huge grin on his face, wondering what he had done to them this time. Eventually he would get tossed into what we called the "Death Ditch" —a steep slope on the edge of the schoolyard covered with thick bushes that often broke his fall—or be dog-piled on by those boys and any other kids who just happened to be in the vicinity.

I asked Larry what he was doing with his life, and he said he was a writer for a fairly new national magazine for teenagers. It was called *Veritas*, the Latin word for "truth." He went on to say that the magazine was Catholic, and that its mission was to present the Catholic faith through the eyes of pop culture. He said there were six other young adults working out of the founders' garage. I knew nothing about the publishing industry, but it sounded very interesting.

Larry soon introduced me to Paul Lauer, who had started the magazine with $3,000 his Jewish grandfather had left him when he died a few years earlier. Like me, Paul had his roots in rock 'n' roll, playing guitar for a band that played all over L.A. On the brink of his band getting very prominent attention, he had a conversion experience after his Irish grandmother had given him a Miraculous Medal just before she died. From there, Paul quit his band, gave up surfing temporarily, and moved out to the desert for two years, living in a shack and reading the Bible and any other religious books he could find. When Paul returned to L.A., he started the magazine out of his parents' garage and felt called to evangelize to the Catholic youth of America.

One day I went to visit this garage in West L.A., where I met Paul briefly and then Joe, the company VP of sorts. He was a tall and jovial Irishman from Michigan who hadn't been in L.A. that long, but had a lot of business sense and a great love for Notre Dame. He would often refer to it as "Our Lady's school." It was a while before I put two and two together to understand that "Notre Dame" *is* French for "Our Lady."

Paul recognized that he needed to fill out the business aspect of his fast-growing company, so Joe was Paul's right-hand man. I then met Seba, an intelligent goth-punker who had earrings everywhere and wore everything black and drank a six-pack of Coke every day. In spite of this intimidating description, he preferred the Latin Mass and all things extremely orthodox within the Catholic Church, and was the controller who handled all the finances for the company. Then there was O.B., a twenty-something typical southern California surfer with handsome looks, blonde hair, and bronze skin. He was the graphic artist who handled the layout of the magazine on his Macintosh. O.B. was somewhat quiet, but he had a devilish sense of humor and did some great impersonations.

Then I met Tom Ehart, the managing editor. He was a transplant from Pennsylvania; he was very thin, with dark hair and skin that made it obvious he didn't spend much time in the sun. He was mild-mannered, soft-spoken and also a musician and singer. His calm personality made him very easy to like. He pointed out their newest office gadget: a fax machine complete with rolls of paper. I had no idea what it did, but I figured I'd learn soon enough.

After I made the rounds and met everyone, Joe wanted to put me to work. I told him briefly about my conversion, and I said I just wanted to serve God in some way. He said there was something I could do. The neighbor next door was nice enough to allow *Veritas* to use their garage for storage. It had become very cluttered with old issues of the magazines, stationery, boxes, and who knows what else. Joe asked if I could clean that portion of the garage so it was more presentable, and organize what I could.

I spent the next two hours doing just that. Joe came back and was extremely happy. I didn't know that was part of the interview, but he said I did such a good job that he wanted to hire me. He said he still had to run it by the boss (Paul) and they had no money to pay me, but not to worry. With so much optimism, what was I to worry about? And so I was hired. It was also about this time they had decided to change the name of the magazine to something simpler and catchy, and thus *YOU!* became the new magazine name, and Veritas Communications was retained as the name of the company.

I was now driving to work from Redondo Beach to West L.A. The commute was grueling. I couldn't see how people could do this day after day for years and years. I had to keep reminding myself this was my way of serving God and to just suck it up, traffic and all. There was no room to put me in the garage with everyone else working on *YOU!* magazine. There were now eight others crammed in there with all kinds of file cabinets, desks, computers, and office equipment. Two girls from Wisconsin and Chicago had just relocated to L.A. to help out. I ended up in a den inside Paul's parents' home, where I could set up a desk, a phone, and work away. Joe had recently decided that because the company was growing and the magazine circulation was expanding, a more professional image was needed. Up until then, it was very "Southern California Casual" in terms of attire. Now, the guys needed to wear long-sleeve dress shirts and ties. It seemed a bit much, but in hindsight, people would stop by for meetings with Paul and Joe, and I can see how they wanted to convey that we were a serious operation. Prominent donors, priests and several of the auxiliary bishops of the L.A. diocese would occasionally stop by, who also served as advisors to the magazine.

Because we were a small outfit, there was no orientation or training, and since everyone was up to their eyeballs in what they needed to do, Joe would give me various tasks and projects on the fly. I helped on marketing campaigns to broaden the reach of *YOU!* magazine and was making phone calls to priests all over the country. It was exciting to see how many priests were already familiar with the magazine and were doing so much to spread the word about it in their parishes.

We all felt we were doing something for a worthy cause. There was no other publication geared toward Catholic teenagers that had inspiring stories of faith and morality written by other young Catholics and Christians. Celebrities and professional athletes were featured, such as Brooke Shields, Isaiah Thomas, Kirk Cameron, John Stamos, Gloria Estefan, Michael W. Smith, Amy Grant, and countless others who we saw as examples of Christian living in a pop-cultured society.

Through my old guitarist friend, Mike, Hedy came back into my life. That's right, the one I had written off two years earlier. Mike's girlfriend at the time was Hedy's best friend. Mike informed me that Hedy had recently graduated with a nursing degree and was living back at home. We met up shortly thereafter and she gave me her new number. After each of us thinking we had been ignored by the other two years before, we realized what had happened and we put it behind us. I just felt that we were somehow meant to be together. Though we had some years of separation along the way, something seemed to bring us back together. I had a few girlfriends along the way, and though I wasn't prepared to take things further with any of them, I felt that I could with Hedy.

There was just one problem now: Hedy had a boyfriend. I prayed to God for them to break up, and guess what? They did! Within a few weeks, we were dating. From there, we became inseparable. We talked about everything, but I often couldn't stop discussing the events at Medjugorje and how they had transformed my life. She had an interest in wanting to know more.

We found ourselves praying the rosary together, and I continued to thank God for bringing Hedy back into my life. Hedy was raised Catholic, went to Mass on Sundays, and had a deep devotion to Mother Mary. Like many young Catholics, she didn't have a great passion for deepening her spirituality, but with my enthusiasm, she became interested and eagerly dug into some of the books I had been reading.

In the fall, I went to visit my friend Matt in Japan for nine days. It was the first time we had seen each other since we separated back in Norway. Matt was an amazing host, introducing me to some great Japanese friends, and we traveled all over southern Japan. I confided to Matt how I was falling for Hedy and told him I felt she was the girl I was going to marry.

Now that I was immersed in this Catholic world, thanks to *Veritas* and *YOU!* magazine, others from our office and I attended numerous conferences throughout California: Marian conferences, pro-life conferences, Medjugorje conferences and so on. These conferences would always have exhibition halls, where we would set up a promotional booth and distribute free copies of our magazines to those in attendance. I was privileged to hear some of the top speakers and theologians of the day discuss subjects of our faith and spirituality: Father Rene Laurentin, Father Ken Roberts, Mark Miravelle, Wayne Weible, and Scott Hahn, to name just a few.

There was a large Catholic convention held at the Anaheim Convention Center across from Disneyland, where *YOU!* magazine had a booth. It brought back a memory of ten years earlier, when I had attended a diocesan-wide youth rally with my school at the same site. With no interest in the religious rally, my friend Pat and I snuck out of the convention, walked across the street, hopped over a fence right after the train had passed, crossed the railroad tracks and made it into the happiest place on Earth, Disneyland. Of course we had no money, and those were the days where you needed a ticket to get on any ride. Despite that, as we walked around the different sections of the park, we were certain we were having a better time than any of our classmates. And we never got caught.

At the Anaheim Convention Center, we happened to have our booth right next to one that was promoting the music of John Michael Talbot. He was, and perhaps still is, the greatest modern-day Catholic recording artist. His music is soothing, inspirational, and hypnotic all at once. Though he grew up Methodist, he discovered the Catholic faith as an adult and converted. He eventually joined the Franciscan order and established a community of celibate brothers and sisters. Our editor, Tom, told me he spoke with him briefly that weekend, and asked him what he appreciated most about the Catholic Church.

Talbot replied, "Its richness."

It's true—the Catholic Church is so vast, and its liturgy reaches the ends of the earth. When you consider that cloistered, contemplative monks and speaking-in-tongues, hands-in-the-air charismatic types belonging to the same church—along with everyone in between—surely there is a place where anybody can feel comfortable in their approach to worshipping God. John Michael

Talbot continues to tour the world and share his beautiful voice and music.

At that same convention, Ivan, the Medjugorje visionary, was in Anaheim along with an archbishop of Croatia to give a talk about his experiences and share the messages of the Blessed Mother. O.B., our graphic designer, had a friend there whose mother knew someone who was taking care of Ivan and his Croatian friends during this visit. This was the "City of Angels", after all, where it came down to who you knew for any kind of inside access. Through this source, we were able to get into to the small room where later that day, at 6:40 p.m., Ivan would have his apparition with only about a dozen others in the room, including the archbishop, John Michael Talbot, and Hedy and I. It was an incredible experience being in that room and watching Ivan converse with the Mother of God. It was peaceful—such a dramatic difference from the top of Cross Mountain a year earlier with thousands of people around. I was so glad Hedy was able to share that moment with me. I was grateful and honored to be in such a place.

As I continued to read, I kept hearing references to a man named Bishop Fulton Sheen. I read his autobiography, *Treasure in Clay*. Afterward, I could understand why many still referred to him as one of the greatest advocates of our faith in the twentieth century. Archbishop Sheen had written more than seventy books in his lifetime and was known as the first televangelist. Before his television career, he had a successful weekly radio program called *The Catholic Hour,* which he hosted for twenty years. He had an audience of more than four million people, and he received between three and six thousand letters a week from listeners. After that, he shifted his focus to two weekly television programs that ran for almost fifteen years. Called *Life is Worth Living* and *The Fulton Sheen Program*, Sheen would reach out to more than thirty million viewers a week and receive more than eight thousand letters a week. It's worth noting that in the mid-1950s, the U.S. population had 40 percent fewer people than today. Even the most-watched primetime television shows these days, such as *American Idol* or *Dancing With the Stars*, are lucky to hit twenty million viewers on a good night!

Fast-forward to the present, and we have a similar Catholic evangelical media mogul in EWTN (Eternal Word Television Network). Founded by Mother Angelica, a nun of the Poor Clares of Perpetual Adoration, in 1981, the network's mission is to utilize the media to spread the Gospel. EWTN has a viewership of more than 140 million people in 127 countries, channeled through five thousand different cable systems, wireless networks, and satellite feeds.

In my bedroom, I had a bookshelf filled with numerous books that belonged to my parents. They were mostly fictional paperbacks and other miscellaneous titles that I never really paid attention to. I came across an old paperback that was quite small. Its edges were browned from the years, and some of the pages had come loose from the binding. Otherwise, it was still readable, despite the mustiness that filled the air around it. The title was *The Seeds of Contemplation* by Thomas Merton. I had never heard of this book nor this author, but somehow I felt compelled to dig into it simply because it seemed so old.

In fact, the edition I was holding was the first edition printed in 1949, and the price was listed at twenty-five cents. I started reading it, and I soon found myself not able to put it down. I found the subject matter and intellect so deep—at least for me—that I often had to stop after several paragraphs to digest what I had just read. It wasn't long before I saw the depth of the spirituality that was Thomas Merton:

"You seem to be the same person, and you are the same person that you have always been: in fact you are more yourself than you have ever been before. You have only just begun to exist. You feel as if you were at last fully born. All that went before was a mistake, a fumbling preparation for birth. Now you have come into your element...you have felt the doors fly open into infinite freedom, into a wealth which is perfect because none of it is yours, and yet it all belongs to you." (From Chapter Twelve, "The Gift of Understanding")

The beauty of Merton's writing mesmerized me. After finishing that book, I wanted more. In Merton's life, he had published more than seventy books, including *The Seven Storey Mountain* and *No Man Is An Island*. As a Trappist monk in Kentucky, he wrote on a variety of subjects, including spirituality, social justice, war, and Eastern mysticism. He even became friends with the Dalai Lama. I soon became one of Thomas Merton's biggest fans, and I found myself reading whatever I could find with his name on it. I also later attended a weekend retreat that was focused on his writings. His writings helped fuse my faith with everything else I was learning.

At the same time, another change was underway. The catechism, or teachings, of the church had last been updated five hundred years earlier. After the Vatican II council in the 1960s and hundreds of years of change within the church, Pope John Paul

II, felt it was time to update those teachings. I couldn't wait to get my copy of the new catechism. I appreciated the pope's efforts to sharpen the focus of what the modern church was all about. I also came to appreciate the unbroken lineage of popes, dating back from Saint Peter as the first head of the church, all the way to our present-day Pope Francis, the 266th pontiff.

At John Paul II's suggestion, an advisory panel of theologians and clergy assembled the documents addressing the major tenets of our faith. This "rough draft" was then sent to all the bishops across the globe, and they would be able to add or modify any aspect of the new catechism as they saw fit, complete with their own notes. The Vatican then collected those drafts. They were scrutinized, edited, and finally used to complete the final text of the new catechism. So, in the end, the leaders of the universal church acted to produce this revised book of teachings.

I was learning about my church, my faith, and along the way, places of Marian apparitions that drew people to them in the same way Medjugorje draws pilgrims today. I took it upon myself to learn as much as I could about these other places where Mary has appeared throughout history.

Lourdes, France and Fatima, Portugal were the most popular, but even growing up, I don't recall ever hearing what made those places special. I obtained books about Our Lady of Guadalupe, Fatima, Lourdes, Garabandal in Spain, and Kibeho in Rwanda. Although Marian apparitions had been happening hundreds of years, it seemed that Mary was appearing more and more frequently in recent years, and her messages were generally the same as in Medjugorje—that of peace and conversion.

The most significant of these stories for me was that of Lourdes. Saint Bernadette Soubirous, the young girl who saw the apparitions at Lourdes, became one of my favorite saints. I read a great biography of Bernadette and watched the movie *Song of Bernadette*. In 1942, the novel, which preceded the film, spent a year on the *New York Times* bestsellers list. The movie based on it won four Oscar awards in 1943, and the following year it won a Golden Globe Award for "Best Motion Picture."

Like the children from Fatima who were also ridiculed and tormented by local authorities, Bernadette was seen as the town lunatic and was tirelessly interrogated by local police and clergy as she tried to explain to the villagers what she was seeing and hearing from the Blessed Mother. Her parents were at a loss and could not bear all the negative attention their daughter was bringing on them.

After several weeks and more than a dozen apparitions in the same place (a grotto known for being the town dump), the final apparition proved to be the one that converted the entire town. Mary had asked Bernadette to drink of the water of the spring and to wash in it. Problem was, there was no spring. Digging in the ground, she began to wash her face with what was just dirt and actually put some in her mouth. Of course, the onlookers in attendance began to mock her, and they walked away feeling their time had been wasted by a mentally unstable girl. However, the following day, it was discovered that water was now flowing from the very spot where Bernadette had dug in the ground. The water has been flowing ever since.

The waters from that spring have proven evidence of healing properties, and numerous miracles have happened to those who have applied those waters to their bodies. There have been sixty-seven miracles officially investigated and authenticated by the

Church in Lourdes; unofficial estimates have put the healings in the thousands. In either case, millions of pilgrims over the years have had their faith affirmed by visiting this shrine, which Mary had asked Bernadette to be built in her honor more than a century ago.

Shortly after the apparitions, Bernadette was called to the religious life and joined the convent of the Sisters of Nevers. The convent life proved to be a true sanctuary for Bernadette, as she did not like the attention now given to her since her fame had spread around the world. She kept a simple life, and would often take care of other sisters who had taken ill. The other sisters would realize much later the suffering Bernadette herself had endured. Having lived with asthma, which seemed to have progressed into tuberculosis, she died at the young age of thirty-five. With great humility, Bernadette had kept her sickness a secret as long as she could so as to not bring any additional attention to herself. Thirty years later, the local bishop had her coffin exhumed to find that her body was still intact and incorrupt.

To this day, it is a miracle that you can still see Bernadette's body in a glass casket on display in the church in Nevers, France. Her body looks very much like it must have the day she died and has shown little signs of corruption. She was declared a saint in 1933. The beautiful lady who appeared to Bernadette proclaimed herself as the "Immaculate Conception," meaning that Mary herself was conceived without sin. Bernadette's visions affirmed what the Church had declared just a short time before the apparitions first began in 1854. At that time, Pope Pius IX approved the Immaculate Conception as one of the four dogmas related to Mary and the Church. This notion of Mary being the Immaculate Conception had been argued for centuries within the Church, and so the apparitions to a poor farm girl who had no knowledge of this Church teaching was as if Mary herself was putting her stamp of approval on what the Church had declared. If Mary had been born with original sin, as we all are, then Jesus' own divinity would have been lessened.

I found out there were many other saints whose bodies were incorrupt like Bernadette. There are books on a number of saints whose bodies you can still see today, even though they have been dead for hundreds of years: Saint Vincent De Paul, Saint John Vianney, Saint Teresa Margaret, Saint John Bosco and even Saint Silvan, who was martyred more than sixteen-hundred years ago. Their bodies have not decomposed. Even the recently deceased Pope John XXIII, who initiated the Second Vatican Council, has a body completely incorrupt.

Hanging out at the Daughters of Saint Paul bookstore in West L.A. gave me the opportunity to discover so much more about this rich faith of mine. Other miracles in the Church were equally fascinating to me, especially ones that pertained to the Eucharist. As Catholics, we literally believe what Jesus says in the sixth chapter of John's gospel: "Whoever eats my flesh and drinks my blood has eternal life, and I will raise him on the last day. For my flesh is true food, and my blood is true drink. Whoever eats my flesh and drinks my blood remains in me and I in him." Sadly, other than the papacy, it is this verse which separates the majority of our other Christian brothers and sisters from the Catholic Church. Jesus is not being symbolic here. It is why we call it "communion" — Jesus is allowing himself to be present to us and in us in the most intimate way. Believing that the bread and wine actually turn into Jesus' body and blood during the consecration of the Mass may seem a bit odd to some, but it is why it is called a "mystery of faith."

I discovered some crazy stories of Eucharistic miracles—of how Communion hosts actually turned into flesh, and wine into blood. Even though some of these miracles date back to the year 700 (in Lanciano, Italy), the flesh and blood is still visible and intact to this day. In Stitch, Bavaria, there occurred a Eucharistic miracle as recently as 1970. Scientific studies have actually affirmed that such tissue, which was physically transformed from the host, was the heart tissue of a certain blood type (AB), was human, and contained no traces of any preservative that would keep the flesh from deteriorating after so many years.

There are also countless accounts of tears, oil, and blood literally flowing from statues of Mary and Jesus in all parts of the world. It seems as if God has been working overtime to get our attention, and there is no shortage of miraculous events we can turn to that inspire our faith. Naturally, there have been many hoaxes throughout the centuries, and the Catholic Church is never too hasty to authenticate something that could be considered supernatural. Even with all of the obvious fruits of religious conversion, healings, and miracles that have occurred in Medjugorje, the Church has yet to take an official stand on the events taking place there, even after thirty years. Its policy is to wait until the event is over before coming out and stating its authenticity, and even afterward, much investigation is required, which can take years. I have come to appreciate that approach and see it as quite fitting. The Vatican will actually play "devil's advocate" with such proclaimed miracles and do everything to investigate the source to prove it false and inconsistent with Church teaching. If there is any aspect of a miracle that goes against Church teaching or tradition, then it is tossed out without a chance of validation. In Hawaii, one of the supposed miracle cures associated with Saint Damien of Molokai was thrown out because the cancer patient had received one dose of radiation. Even though the cancer went into complete remission, because of that one dose the Vatican denied any divine intervention in that case. The Vatican did approve a separate miracle later, however, which contributed to the cause for Father Damien's canonization.

Through my conversion, I came to realize that I didn't know much about my faith. I discovered that our Christian Catholic faith embodies so much history and diversity. With at least a couple of hundred various religious orders around the world that range from complete monasticism to ones that are active in mass media (Daughters of Saint Paul) and education (the Jesuits), there truly is something for everybody. And then there are the different Catholic rites. I never knew that most of the rites within the Catholic faith actually have roots dating back to the first apostles.

I was familiar, of course, with the Roman or Latin rite. Later, I found out there existed other Eastern Catholic rites such as the Byzantine, Alexandrian (Coptic), Syriac, Armenian, Maronite, and Chaldean Rites, which are in communion with Rome and the universal Church at large. The Syrian rite traces its roots back to Saint James the Apostle. Saint Mark the Apostle was the founder of the Alexandrian rite, which has a following today among the Coptic Christians in Egypt. The Chaldeans trace their history back to Saint Thomas, and are found mostly in India. The Byzantine rite is found throughout Russia, Belarus, Bulgaria, Albania, Croatia, Slovakia, Romania, and Ukraine.

Though there may have been some divisions along the way, in time these rites were recognized as fully valid. These also happened to be some of the first areas to be influenced by Christianity as it gained ground around the world. *The Catechism of the Catholic Church* states, "The celebration of the liturgy, therefore, should correspond to the genius and culture of the different peoples. In order that the mystery of Christ be 'made known to all the nations...to bring about the obedience of faith,' it must be proclaimed, celebrated and lived in all cultures in such a way that they themselves are not abolished by it, but redeemed and fulfilled." It was interesting to find out that in Lebanon today, even though the populations of those who practice the Maronite rite are a minority, it is in the country's statute—going back to the fourth century—that the president of the country be a Maronite.

As these rites have continued over the centuries in the Middle East and the Balkans, a wave of Roman Catholicism is sweeping across Africa and Asia, the newer territories of growth for the Church. At the beginning of the twentieth century, sub-Saharan Africa had two million Catholics. Now there are more than 130 million. From 2000 to 2008, the number of Catholics grew by 33 percent in Africa and 15 percent in Asia. In Seoul, South Korea, there are more than two hundred Catholic parishes. To put in perspective the explosive growth in South Korea, the entire country had just 250 priests in 1960. Today there are more than five thousand, and more than two-thirds of the priests are under the age of forty. The number of South Korean Catholics has grown from three million to greater than five million in just the last ten years. (Vatican Statistical Report 2010)

Someone who did their part in spreading the Gospel to the multitudes was also one of the most remarkable modern-day saints who had the ability to read souls: Padre Pio. As a young priest he obtained the stigmata, or the wounds of Christ, and bore them for more than fifty years, almost until the day he died.

A Capuchin priest in Italy, his motto was simple: "Pray, hope and be happy." Padre Pio often said, "Through the study of books, one seeks God; through meditation, one finds God." He was known to have the gift of bi-location, the ability to physically be in two places at once. He also had the ability to heal, speak in tongues, survive only on the Eucharist for days at a time, manage on just a few hours of sleep, and was known for spending up to fourteen hours in the confessional. He would endure spiritual and physical battles with the devil and demons, in which he would be thrown about his room and have furniture tossed on him. His body would later show serious wounds and cuts that he endured at the hands of the evil one. The devil would sometimes appear as young, naked girls dancing around him, while at other times the devil would disguise himself as Jesus, Mary, Joseph, or his guardian angel, with whom Padre Pio would also have personal visions and communications. However, he could always distinguish the devil, and with the intercession of Jesus, his guardian angel, and Mary, the devil would disappear.

Padre Pio had a tremendous love for the Mass, but he will for certain be known most for having the wounds of Christ, which he bore all those years with great humility and sacrifice. Though he rarely showed it, he was filled with pain on a daily basis and was also embarrassed by the stigmata, which caused him to visibly bleed from his hands and side. Several days before he died in 1968, all evidence of the bleeding disappeared. He was canonized a saint in 2002 by Pope John Paul II, who in 1947 had actually visited Padre Pio and had his confession heard by him at the time.

The lives of all the saints are inspirational, but the miracles that surrounded them are really secondary to their level of spirituality, which was at the root of anything supernatural they may have accomplished. It has been said that a saint is an ordinary person who did extraordinary things. Many were simple people who led humble lives. They had an incredible love for God that made them pious examples. Some, like Saint Francis of Assisi, were wealthy and had great fortunes. However, they were spiritually void, and recognized that in giving up these treasures, they could deepen their love of God and find a richness in being poor and serving those in need. These are true models for any age and time. Their stories are diverse, which is why they are so relatable. We can connect with their desire to achieve a greater closeness to God. Often these saints led lives hardly worthy of the Kingdom, and it was their conversion experience that awakened them to a new reality—a life in Christ, a life meaningless without him. Jesus became their "all in all," and they lived their lives on that premise alone.

The common threads running through the lives of the saints are love and service to others, which became the premise for their being. That is also the legacy the Church wishes to impart on the faithful—that through the examples of the saints, we too may desire to love and be of service to one another. That, to me, is the meaning of life: love and service, plain and simple. Love God, love your neighbor, put on a servant's heart, and give to those around you the time, talent, and treasure God has blessed you with. After all, that is what the message of the Gospel is, the message that Jesus came to give us while he lived out his earthly ministry.

Life can be so complicated sometimes, so much so that it can be easy to overlook the simplicity of this message. But it is one we need to be reminded of—one that *I* need to be reminded of—on a regular basis. I can plead that I'm not worthy, but then again, who among us is? What makes it more challenging is that once this truth is evident, you cannot hide from it. No longer can I plead ignorant, as much as I may want to. It is said, "To whom much is given, much is required." When "given" this faith and understanding, one is expected to live that out as a Christian should. However, that is not always so easy. We fall short sometimes.

It is, and should be, a universal message. It transcends religion, politics, economics, and culture, and yet it can transform each of these areas just the same. It can be said that Gandhi's nonviolent message of love and respect of others not only gained independence for his entire country of India, but also united Muslims, Hindus, Jews, and Christians, who traditionally had deep divisions with one another. Gandhi's example of love and service actually shaped the political and religious landscape of India, not to mention its culture. However, in the Balkans in the early '90s, trouble was stirring, and an ethnic division of hate would soon sweep across that region.

Chapter 6

REVOLUTION

"Dear Children! Today I invite you to pray for peace. At this time peace is being threatened in a special way, and I am seeking from you to renew fasting and prayer in your families. Dear children, I desire you to grasp the seriousness of the situation and that much of what will happen depends on your prayers and you are praying a little bit. Dear children, I am with you and I am inviting you to begin to pray and fast seriously as in the first days of my coming. Thank you for having responded to my call."

Medjugorje Message, July 25, 1991

The Yugoslav war began to rage between the Serbs (Eastern Orthodox), Bosnians (Muslim), and Croatians (Catholics). It was clear the messages coming out of Medjugorje took on a more serious tone and were trying to warn us of this impending tragedy. For decades, Muslims, Serbs, and Catholics lived together with a tremendous amount of tolerance and respect for each other's beliefs. They may have had their differences, but overall they had learned to live with and among each other. Most would not have thought that a civil war would be possible.

It started out as more of a territorial war than a religious one after areas of Yugoslavia began declaring their independence. At *Veritas*, we knew people who lived there, and we would periodically hear from them via fax and letter about the atrocities. The level of torture and genocide and ethnic cleansing was the worst it had been since World War II, and I could not believe the stories that were coming out of the Balkans.

Entire villages were wiped out. I kept thinking that it couldn't be long before Medjugorje would be affected. I received a letter from the Vrbanec family, who had to leave their home in a rush and go to live with relatives in Split, some hours away from Mostar. I remember seeing a picture of the historic arched Mostar bridge, which was centuries old, but had been damaged beyond use. Its famous arch had become nothing but two stubs of concrete coming out of the sides of the riverbanks, and its mid-section was blown away. I had walked over that bridge in my visits with Nela and Tony.

My family and friends sent money and clothes to them. It wasn't until 2000 that I received an email from the Vrbanec's son, Josef. The email contained a number of pictures from their Mostar home. There was no roof or windows, and the home looked like it had been bombed. With the amount of rape and murder running rampant, they were lucky to get out alive.

We were astonished that there was little response from the U.S. or the international community. The United Nations' Green

Zones, established for those who had been displaced, was over-run by the Serbs. There was no respect for any rules of war, and nothing was off limits—churches, mosques, historic buildings, and the like were bombed, set on fire, and left to burn. Civilians were often the targets, and for three cold winters, those who could not escape their cities would risk their lives to go outside amidst sniper fire to forage for grass and to eat dirt. To survive bombs and bullets, families huddled in tiny bathrooms away from the windows of their homes. It is said that up to two-hundred thousand people were killed in those several years, and many more were wounded. We had heard that Medjugorje became a refuge for soldiers, and despite being so close to the danger zone, the town was miraculously spared any serious damage.

Another famous Marian apparition of Our Lady in Kibeho, Rwanda, also began in 1981. To this day, it is the only Marian apparition in Africa approved by the Vatican, made official in 2001. Her apparitions were to seven young children—one who was not even Christian, but an illiterate pagan boy who had never seen a Bible, much less been in a church. As in Medjugorje, Mary predicted a great war if people did not convert to God, and the visionaries there were shown images of bodies being hacked to death and a river of blood running through their villages. A little more than ten years later, this prophecy would be fulfilled in Rwanda, as Hutus waged war on the Tutsis, killing roughly a million people in just one hundred days, the weapon of choice being the machete. What is hard to believe is that many Hutus and Tutsis shared the same Christian and Catholic faiths, and yet once war was declared and ethnic cleansing began, no place was secure. Even Catholic churches, filled with frightened women and children, were peppered with gunfire, and then machetes were taken to those who did not fall in the hail of bullets. As in Bosnia, the international response was too little too late, and in the end, almost twenty percent of the Tutsi population was decimated.

Thanks to movies like *Hotel Rwanda*, there are a few glimpses of good that could be found among the tragedy, including an incredible testimony by Immaculee Ilibagiza, who was almost killed herself had it not been for a Protestant pastor who provided sanctuary to her and six other women in a small bathroom for three months, where they almost starved to death. Her faith strengthened when most people's would have faltered, and she not only survived, but somehow found it in her heart to forgive those who had persecuted her, including the men who killed her two brothers and parents. The story of forgiveness told in her book *Left To Tell: Discovering God Amidst the Rwandan Holocaust* would become a *New York Times* bestseller. As terrible as these wars were, there was an even greater war being waged with many more casualties within our own border—a war pitting a mother against her own child in the womb.

Within You Without You

Along with all my spiritual reading, I read Pope Paul VI's papal encyclical, *Humanae Vitae*. I had heard of it before, and I knew it to be about the sanctity of life, but nothing more. I was moved by the beauty of his words. It affirmed the Catholic doctrine for me that we are to protect and preserve ALL human life, from conception to natural death, and the consequences of artificial birth control were important for every Catholic to understand. This was not a new teaching in as much as it was affirming what the Church had stood for all along. The timing was necessary, however, given the rise of Planned Parenthood clinics, the contraceptive pill and the decline in sexual morality. This issue needed to be addressed again. *Humanae Vitae* states, "It is to be anticipated that perhaps not everyone will easily accept this particular teaching (regarding consequences of artificial birth control). There is too much clamorous outcry against the voice of the Church, and this is intensified by modern means of communication. But it comes as no surprise to the Church that she, no less than her divine Founder, is destined to be a 'sign of contradiction.' (22) She does not, because of this, evade the duty imposed on her of proclaiming humbly but firmly the entire moral law, both natural and evangelical." (*Humanae Vitae 18*)

The Catechism of the Catholic Church states, "Human life is sacred because from its beginning it involves the creative action of God and it remains forever in a special relationship with the Creator, who is its sole end. God alone is the Lord of Life from its beginning until its end: no one can under any circumstance claim for himself the right directly to destroy an innocent human being." Not only is the Fifth Commandment quite clear in stating that "You shall not kill" (Exodus 20:13), but in Exodus 23:7 it states, "Do not slay the innocent and the righteous." The Catechism goes on to say that, "Human life must be respected and protected absolutely from the moment of conception. From the first moment of his existence, a human being must be recognized as having the rights of a person—among which is the inviolable right of every innocent being to life."

To me, there was something very disturbing about a mother taking the life of her own child. That seemed to go against all things natural, yet millions do it each year. And how do doctors not have the moral sense to see that what they are doing is wrong? The 1973 Supreme Court decision legalizing abortion in the United States has only complicated the issue.

Over the years, it seems the argument has been about what rights a mother has, while any rights of a baby's father, aunts, uncles, and grandparents are ignored. The welfare of the mother is put ahead of everyone else, and few put any value on the precious life living inside the womb. When I was growing up, California condor eggs were given greater status and attention than the innocent lives lost in human wombs due to abortion.

I tried to educate myself about this issue as much as I could by reading about both sides—those pro-life, and those proclaiming themselves as pro-choice. Four decades later, do we even remember how legalized abortion came about? I learned that the real name of "Jane Roe" (from the Supreme Court decision to legalize abortion in all fifty states, *Roe v. Wade*) was Norma McCorvey. When McCorvey was pregnant, she was sought after by the pro-choice propagandists to endorse legalized abortion across the nation. McCorvey was a strong supporter of women's rights and thought her pro-choice friends were on her side.

The landmark case began in 1970 when her friends advised her to falsely assert that she had been raped so she would then be eligible to obtain a legal abortion (with the understanding that Texas' anti-abortion laws allowed abortions in the cases of rape). Police evidence was lacking, so the scheme was unsuccessful, and McCorvey would later admit the story was a fabrication. She attempted to obtain an illegal abortion, but authorities closed down the clinics. Eventually, McCorvey was referred to two female attorneys. The case took three years of trials to reach the U.S. Supreme Court. In the meantime, McCorvey had given birth to the baby in question, and later gave it up for adoption.

McCorvey revealed herself to be "Jane Roe" of the decision within days of its issuance and stated that she had sought an abortion because she was unemployable and greatly depressed.

In time, the truth of what had transpired came out, and in the 1980s, McCorvey asserted in her book, *Won by Love*, that she had been the "pawn" of two young and ambitious lawyers who were looking for a plaintiff with whom they could challenge the Texas state law prohibiting abortion. In effect, the Supreme Court ruling overturned every state law against abortion and entailed a "right to privacy," which allowed women to procure an abortion. It's hard to believe that one of the most historic decisions by the U.S. Supreme Court was based on a lie by the plaintiff. In 1998, after several years of Catholic instruction about the faith, Norma McCorvey was received into the Catholic Church. She was by then very much a part of the pro-life movement, as she remains to this day.

Another important ruling by the Supreme Court was *Doe v. Bolton*. The court ruled that abortion for "the health of the mother" could not be restricted, while adopting a very broad definition of what "may relate to health," including "all factors—physical, emotional, psychological, familial, and the women's age—relevant to the well-being of the patient." This effectively made abortion legal through all nine months of pregnancy for almost any reason. *Source:* Doe v. Bolton, *410 U.S. 179 (1973).*

The "Mary Doe" in *Doe v. Bolton* was Sandra Cano. She had gone to a free legal clinic seeking help to get a divorce and retrieve her children from foster care. She happened to be pregnant at the time. You may wonder how this could ever happen, but without her realizing what they were doing, her lawyers sidelined the issues she wanted help with and instead filed a lawsuit stating that she wanted an abortion. When Cano's mother and lawyer arranged for her to have an abortion, she fled the state.

Unfortunately, Cano did not understand the legal jargon being used in her case. She had no idea that her lawyers were fighting for abortion rights, not for her divorce. Cano has always been and continues to be opposed to abortion. Cano even filed a motion for the Supreme Court to rehear and overturn her case, but in 2006, the Court refused. That's right, the U.S. Supreme Court got duped again. Her story is chronicled in the book *Supreme Deception*. (*Source: Fletcher Lash, Sybil. 2002.* Supreme Deception: How an Activist Attorney Manipulated the U.S. Supreme Court and Gave Birth To Partial Birth Abortions. *Lawrenceville: Sentinel Productions.*)

Norma McCorvey and Sandra Cano were not the only ones who came over to the side of life. While I was working at *YOU!* magazine, someone had given me a cassette tape. On it was a powerful testimony of a doctor who had performed thousands of abortions. This gave me an inside view of how the abortion industry worked.

The late Dr. Bernard Nathanson was responsible for more than seventy thousand abortions, five thousand by his own hands. Based in New York City, his clinic was the largest provider of abortions in the Western World. He was even responsible for aborting his own child, which he would come to later regret. Dr. Nathanson was the director of the National Abortion Rights Action League (NARAL). In the 1970s, they were instrumental in getting the pro-choice movement into the mainstream and inflaming the myths that a child in the womb is simply an inhuman blob of tissue, and that a mother's "right of privacy" allowed her to have complete control over her own body. Unable to deny the science of what takes place in the womb thanks in part to ultrasound technology coming about in 1976, Dr. Nathanson later gave up his practice and became ardently pro-life and one of the most outspoken critics of abortion. In 1984, he would direct and narrate a movie called *Silent Scream*, which showed an actual abortion taking place via ultrasound. The film was widely distributed to schools, churches, and even to all members of Congress at President Ronald Reagan's request. Although he was raised Jewish, Dr. Nathanson would eventually convert to Catholicism in 1996.

When you take the time to truly comprehend the beauty of life in the womb, I can't understand how anyone could see it as anything else other than a miracle. That moment of fertilization when a baby's DNA is established is not just backed up by the teachings of the Church, but by science as well. The beginning of a human life is truly a miracle that only a mighty and powerful God can make a reality.

Reading bestselling author Og Mandino's *The Greatest Miracle in the World,* I was reminded of the complexity of our bodies, which hold a host of miracles that modern science has revealed. Our bodies contain more than five hundred muscles, two hundred bones, and seven miles of nerve fibers. The eyes hold one hundred million receptors, and each ear holds twenty-four thousand nerves. Our hearts beat thirty-six million times per year. In that year, they pump more than seven-hundred thousand gallons of blood through sixty thousand miles of veins, arteries, and tubing. Our lungs filter oxygen through six-hundred million pockets of folded flesh.

Within the five quarts of our blood, there are more than twenty trillion blood cells; within each cell, there are millions of molecules; and within each molecule is an atom oscillating at more than ten million times *each second.* Two million of your blood cells die every single second, and they are quickly replaced by two million more. The brain has more than thirteen billion nerve cells to help file away every perception, sound, taste, smell, and action you have ever experienced. Within each cell are more than a billion protein molecules. The communication network in your brain can perform twenty-million billion calculations per second. Your body has more than four million pain-sensitive structures, five-hundred thousand touch detectors, and more than two-hundred thousand temperature detectors.

Og Mandino goes on to state that, "Each of us arrived from two cells united in a miracle. Each cell containing twenty-three chromosomes and within each chromosome hundreds of genes, which would govern every characteristic about you, from the color of your eyes to the charm of your manner, to the size of your brain. Beginning with that single sperm from your father's four-hundred million, through the hundreds of genes in each of the chromosomes from your mother and father, God could have created three-hundred-thousand billion humans, each different from the other. But who did God bring forth?"

You and only you!

Chapter 7

With a little help from my friends

On May 19, 1991—my parents' 35th wedding anniversary—I proposed to Hedy. We were married six months later. It was made official and sacramental by our friend, Father Ferraro. My parents came all the way from Fiji for our wedding and met their new daughter-in-law for the first time. Matt, my best man, came from Japan to give the toast, which dragged on just long enough for the champagne to almost go flat. Love you, Matt!

Veritas Communications had recently relocated to Agoura Hills, about an hour outside of L.A. The drive was tiring me each day, so right after we married I moved out of my parents' house, and Hedy and I began our new life together renting an apartment in nearby Westlake Village. It was nice to be out of the big city and nestled among large rolling hills scattered with oak trees. On the other side of the grassy hills through the canyon was Malibu, where, on occasion, we would take scenic drives into L.A. along the Pacific Coast Highway to visit Hedy's family in Torrance.

On Christmas Day in 1991, something astounding happened. After decades of anxiety and generations of civilians living in fear of each other, the Cold War ended. Communism would be over in the Soviet Union, and neither would exist anymore. Years of oppression and economic hardships were lifted from the citizens who lived there, and they could finally live a life they had only dreamed about. Just a couple of weeks earlier on the feast of Mary's Immaculate Conception (December 8), the leaders of Russia, Ukraine, and Belarus signed an accord to dissolve the Soviet Union. It went into effect on the feast day of Jesus' birth, which we were now witnessing in our living room as the Russian citizens celebrated and cheered in the streets of Saint Petersburg, formerly Leningrad. To me, none of this was coincidence.

On July 13, 1917, Mary appeared a third time to visionaries Jacinta, Lucy, and Francisco in Fatima, Portugal. In addition to predicting World War II, she asked the shepherd children to pray for the conversion of Russia and to consecrate it to her Immaculate Heart. This apparition was four months before the Bolshevik Revolution transformed all of Russia into a communist and atheistic state for the next seven decades.

Fast forward to 1981. Many of us remember the attempted assassination of Pope John Paul II on May 13 of that year—the feast day and anniversary of the Fatima apparitions. He lost almost three-quarters of his blood that day, but later credited his survival of the assassin's four bullets to the Blessed Mother. On March 25, 1984, Pope John Paul II consecrated the whole world and Russia to the Immaculate Heart of Mary. This was the first time it was consecrated with full communion of the bishops worldwide. On the anniversary of the Fatima apparitions in 1984, just two months after the consecration, one of the largest crowds gathered at the shrine to pray the rosary for peace. Then, things began to unravel back in the Soviet Union.

On that same day of prayer, a large accidental explosion occurred at the Soviet Severomorsk Naval Base, which wiped out two-thirds of all the missiles stockpiled for their Northern Fleet. Western military experts called it the worst disaster the Soviet Navy faced since World War II. Later that same year, the Soviet leader Konstantin Chernenko would die. Then in March of 1985, Mikhail Gorbachev would be elected.

A year later, the Chernobyl disaster would bring the Soviet nuclear program to its knees, and May 1988 saw the destruction of a Ukrainian factory that made rocket motors for the Soviets' deadly SS-24 long-range missiles, which could carry ten nuclear bombs each. Then, on August 29, 1989, just several weeks after my first visit to Medjugorje, Sister Lucia, the sole surviving Fatima visionary, sent written correspondence affirming that the complete consecration "had been accomplished" and that "God had kept His word."

The Berlin Wall fell November 9 of that year, and the peaceful revolutions of Czechoslovakia, Romania, Bulgaria, and Albania followed. The year 1990 brought the unification of East and West Germany, and finally, without bloodshed, the entire Soviet Union collapsed—on Christmas Day, to top it off. Hedy and I lived ten minutes from the Ronald Reagan Library, which we took time to visit on a couple of occasions. Displayed on the grounds of the library is a large section of the Berlin Wall to commemorate the part Reagan played in pressing Mikhail Gorbachev to tear down the wall that divided East and West Germany.

Watching world history take place before our eyes was astounding, especially with regards to the prophetic nature of Mary's prior apparitions and messages relating to these events. Unfortunately, in April 1992 we would watch another event unfold. We watched in disbelief as the entire city of L.A. became a riot zone after the Rodney King verdict. Though we were sheltered in the suburbs of Thousand Oaks, it was still close enough for us to realize that L.A. was not a place where we wanted to raise our kids. I had already had enough of the crime, smog, and traffic. After watching Los Angeles burn for a week and seeing the worst in human nature, living anywhere else was going to be an improvement. We began to discuss moving out of state.

It wasn't long before Hedy became pregnant. Several months into the pregnancy, we went to have our first ultrasound. There she was, this little human the size of a peanut swimming around in Hedy's womb. I could see her tiny heart beating and make out her head, body, and limbs. It was an amazing feeling to know this was my child and I was now a father.

After telling us that the baby appeared to be healthy, the doctor said, "Now if this wasn't planned, I can make arrangements for its termination."

"Termination?" I said. What the hell was he talking about? Here we are, a newly married couple sharing in the joy of this new life that we were seeing for the very first time through this amazing technology of ultrasound, and the first thing he thinks about is how he can kill it? I was absolutely stunned with his level of insensitivity.

I said, "No, thank you, we'll be just fine," and walked out of his office. Hedy and I fired that doctor. We found an OB/GYN who was not an abortionist and who was pro-life. He ended up delivering our daughter, and we were grateful to have a doctor who valued life as we did.

Our blessing from above, Camille Marie, was born in March of 1993. Setting eyes on her the moment she was born was one of the most incredible experiences of my life. After the shock of seeing her head full of red hair—my wife and I both have brown—the emotions started seeping in. Nine months were nowhere near long enough to prepare for this moment. Words simply cannot express the emotions that a father feels at that time. A grace of bonding is established for all of eternity. Silently, I revamped John Lennon's, "I Am the Walrus" lyrics to, "I am she (Camille) as you (Hedy) are she (Camille) as you (both) are me and we are all together." Suddenly, it didn't sound so ridiculous.

When she was a baby, I'd often sing her to sleep with the songs "Til There Was You" and "Goodnight" in my finest Paul and Ringo serenading voice. It worked every time, though Camille is probably much better off for not being able to remember me singing to her.

As if having a new baby wasn't enough of a change for us, Hedy and I decided to make a move. I convinced Hedy that Seattle could be a good fit for us, and after a short visit there, we made up our minds. The natural beauty of the Northwest would be a welcome change, I said. Camille was three months old when we relocated to the land of Starbucks, Costco, and Microsoft. We said our goodbyes to family and the Veritas crew and settled into Seattle, where I found a job selling life insurance.

I'd hammer out long days on the weekends to allow me to have a few days off in a row during the week. We took long drives around

Washington with Camille to go on hikes and explore waterfalls and the great outdoors. We loved traveling to Vancouver and seeing that spectacular Canadian city. I made four separate trips to Alaska to sell insurance up there and managed to do some sightseeing. I'll never forget the Northern Lights that I saw many times over.

When I came home from one of my Alaska trips, Hedy had baked a huge heart-shaped cookie the size of a pie that said, "Do you have room in your heart for another?" Being a typical guy, I didn't quite get it at first. Then it dawned on me—she was pregnant again!

After only a year and a half in Seattle, I took a promotion to open my own insurance office in Asheville, North Carolina. We had left L.A. to get away from smog, traffic, crime, and gangs. What we found in Seattle were smog, traffic, crime, and gangs, but many more trees. We loved the trees, but everything else was enough to consider relocating across the country. Within days of Hedy giving birth to our second child, Andrew Joseph, or "AJ" as he's often called now, we were off to our new home near the Blue Ridge Parkway. Hedy flew there with my mom and the kids, while my dad and I drove our belongings across the country.

Driving across the country with Dad was uneventful, but now that I was married and had two children, I thought it was a good opportunity to get to know Dad a little better. Life had moved quickly from when he and Mom were in the Peace Corps, and with Hedy being a part of my life and moving out of state, it felt like we needed to catch up on things. I was five years older and on a very different maturity plane than before, and we had some great conversations as we traversed the country.

Hedy and I bought our first home in Asheville and, in an interesting turn of events, had most of my side of the family within a couple of hours' drive. Mom and Dad had recently retired to South Carolina and built their dream home. My oldest brother Dave and his family had relocated to Charlotte to work for the airlines and had already been there several years. My other brother Dan moved down from Maine with his wife and son to come work with me selling insurance in Asheville. Living in that part of the south was beautiful, and the four seasons were something Hedy and I had never experienced. Arriving in late October made us right on schedule for the peaking of the fall colors. I thought I had died and gone to heaven. Next to a summer in Seattle, it was one of the most beautiful and breathtaking sights of my life, being surrounded by hills covered in various hues of orange, yellow, brown, and gold.

Running my own agency was extremely time-consuming. Sundays were my only day off, and during the week I would often not get home until 9 or 10 p.m. The business consumed me, and I couldn't wait to get home to be with Hedy and the kids. We went to Mass each Sunday, but that was about the extent of our spiritual nourishment and my drums were collecting dust.

There was great promise for me in upper management, so I kept chasing that carrot. Like most things, it was gradual. I felt I was slipping behind from where I was before in my relationship with God. I rationalized that I was married now and had two kids to help take care of, and my role as a provider needed to take center stage. From the beginning, it was our goal to have Hedy stay home with the kids before they began school. This was a luxury most couples simply couldn't afford. We were able to manage that, but it meant my working all the time. We felt at home at the Catholic Church there and made some friends after a while, but after two years, work was simply taking its toll, and most of my spiritual reading came to a standstill.

A nice break came when The Beatles released their *Anthology* book and music chronicling their career. It provided not only some new music from the Fab Four, but also included takes of various songs that had never been released before. The made-for-TV film was a much-publicized event, which I watched and soaked in.

In 1970, each Beatle had gone his separate solo way, and they endured years of legal bickering with one another, with John and Paul being most at odds. Any kind of Beatles reunion seemed remote. It was a bit hypocritical that they couldn't quite be the example of the peace and love that was evident in so many of their songs. Sadly, with John's death, there never would be any true Beatles reunion.

With the passing of time and the release of *Anthology*, we saw an older George, Paul, and Ringo. More than anything else, we saw three childhood friends who were reminded of having experienced something nobody else ever did. With decades having passed since Beatlemania, they had matured enough to understand how much they had shared in it together, and that collective appreciation of what they accomplished so long ago was—and still is—very relevant. So many had written about the Beatles. It was time they themselves looked back on those days from the '60s and told the world what had really happened from their own personal perspective. Filmed from their respective homes, they were relaxed in the presence of each other's company—relaxed enough to play some music while sharing tea together for the first time in who knows how long. This *Anthology* was a historic and beautiful account of the world's greatest band coming to terms with themselves, their relationships with one another, and their legacy.

Speaking of legacy, in June 1995, we went to Charlotte one weekend. My nephew, Nicholas, had just been born, and so not only were we there to see him and my brother and sister-in-law, but also Mother Teresa. She was there to formally open up one of her Sisters of Charity houses in Charlotte. While there, she spoke at the Charlotte Coliseum in front of thousands of people. We were fortunate to have gotten tickets, and it really was a family affair. My brother was there, as were Mom and Dad and, of course, Hedy, Camille, and Andrew.

Mother Teresa spoke for a good hour about the work her sisters were doing in this country and around the world. About half of her talk was focused on love and on the evils of abortion. She did not sugarcoat anything. She was so full of conviction and firm in her belief and not ashamed to talk about it. She encouraged adoption, and even said that she and her sisters would take in any baby and raise it rather than see it aborted.

We have such a great example in Mother Teresa, who looked beyond religion and sought to help the poorest of the poor in Calcutta. Here, a Catholic nun literally took to the streets of the slums to serve in an area predominantly Hindu, loving them and serving them regardless of what they believed.

She was a nun who in 1946 received a "call within a call," and believed that she was meant to serve in a place other than her current convent in Loreto, located near Calcutta, India. After serving nearly twenty years with the Sisters of Loreto and becoming the order's headmistress, in 1950, at the age of forty, she began to serve the poor people of Calcutta. She started a new religious order, the Missionaries of Charity, approved by the Vatican, with only a handful of nuns serving those who were sick and dying around her.

At the time of her death in 1997, she had four thousand nuns serving in her order and had established 610 mission houses in 123 countries serving tens of thousands of people. This is the power of one individual who chose to follow God's call and was able to build a spiritual empire that nobody could have imagined. It would seem impossible, yet this is the power of what God can accomplish through those who commit to him and give their love and service to others.

However, one must not overlook how all this success came to fruition. Seeing an image of Mother Teresa praying in front of the tabernacle or praying the rosary, or simply contemplating in silence while staring at the crucifix is important because this is where she gained the strength to accomplish what she did in a span of fifty years. This is what we must remember about her. She had a deep spirituality and a deep connection to Jesus, which is what gave her purpose. Her mission would not have been successful had she not relied on God to provide her with the people, the resources, and the funding to establish the homes that were built to serve others. Mother Teresa, like all the saints before her, was a woman of prayer—a woman of spiritual longing, a woman who sought to divert attention away from herself and let only God be recognized for any good being done.

After two years of establishing an agency in North Carolina, the opportunity came up to manage another office. I was given twenty minutes to decide if I wanted to go and three weeks to get there. This time it was in Hawaii, on the island of Oahu. North Carolina was nice, but we were missing the coastal lifestyle. It was January 1997 when we arrived in Kailua, and the kids were barely two and three years old. My brother, Dan, had become one of my most consistent producers, and we worked well together. He was looking forward to relocating with me to Oahu, and we formed a partnership and became successful managers our first year in the Islands. We enjoyed selling insurance and built and managed a team of agents. I wished I had partnered with my brother back in Asheville, because it gave me much more time—and a life. Going to clients' homes and selling to the locals gave us a keen insight into the culture and livelihood of Hawaii that would have otherwise taken much longer.

A special road trip came when my brother Dan and I went to the island of Molokai for a week to sell to the prospects there. It was known as the "Friendly Isle," and sure enough, we met the friendliest people there . Having sold insurance in several states now, I could say that having the insurance man over was typically not the highlight of any prospect's week. In fact, getting an appointment without them no-showing became quite an art. On Molokai, however, people welcomed us with open arms as if we were family. It was an awesome experience. We did very well—so well that I went back several times afterward. It was surprising to me that so many were underinsured, and quite a few were without any insurance at all. It was always a comfort to know they were a bit more protected than when we had arrived.

On my second trip to Molokai, I sold a policy to a guy named Kawika. He was one of the mule guides who took people down to Kalaupapa, the peninsula where Father Damien lovingly served those affected by leprosy. The thought occurred to me that since I was so close, I really should try to visit that special place. I knew you couldn't just show up to Kalaupapa—you needed an invite. Kawika assured me that if I showed up the next day, he would be my escort. Early the next morning, I drove up to the topside of the peninsula and met Kawika as he was preparing the mules for the guests who would be riding down that day. I'm allergic to horses and mules, so he said I'd be okay to walk down ahead of their group.

It was an exciting journey, and the scenery was spectacular. Toward the end of the trail my legs were burning, and I wondered how I could possibly hike back up later in the day. There are dozens of switchbacks, and because of the constant pressure, my knees and shins became very sore. I finally made it down to the bottom and waited for Kawika's group to catch up. Once there, he was able to secure a tour pass for me to visit this former leper colony.

The flat peninsula that juts out from the cliffs, known as Kalaupapa, is surrounded on three sides by the Pacific. I was not expecting it to look as beautiful as it did. The land was green, and the ocean was a beautiful blue with constant trade winds blowing. The three-thousand-foot vertical cliffs surrounding the peninsula were the tallest natural prison walls imaginable. I boarded a small bus that took myself and other tourists to the windward side of the peninsula, where Father Damien had first tried to establish some shelter and housing for those afflicted with leprosy when he arrived in 1873. He built Saint Philomena church in Kalawao, and it still stands with numerous tombstones surrounding it, including his own. I tried to imagine what life was like back in his time.

Father Damien's body was exhumed in 1936 and taken back to his homeland of Belgium to remain with his religious order. In 1995, his order, the Congregation of the Sacred Hearts of Jesus and Mary, gave back his right hand to be placed once again in the Kalaupapa tomb where he had first been laid to rest.

Eight thousand Hansen's patients were sent to Kalaupapa in a hundred-year time span up until 1969. The peninsula is one large graveyard, because most patients never left there. Our group met several people afflicted with the disease who worked in the bookstore. They greeted us with warm smiles, but wore dark shades because of the effects of the disease on their vision. We were told there were seventy patients who had chosen to live out their lives on Kalaupapa. Now just a few remain, and they all are in their later years.

Father Damien did so much for the residents of Kalaupapa in dressing their wounds, helping to build homes, educating their children, and forming a band, in addition to providing for their emotional and spiritual needs. He was a superb carpenter, and he even built several churches on the topside of Molokai that still stand today. He built coffins, dug graves, and developed ways to bring water to the residents. Most of all, he gave them a dignity that was all but lost before he arrived.

He was an amazing man and very much deserves to be considered among the ranks of the saints. I also saw where Mother Marianne Cope, a notable Franciscan nun, was buried. I didn't know much about her at the time, other than the fact that she had taken over Father Damien's ministry as his health was failing. He later died from leprosy himself. Unlike Father Damien, Mother Marianne and her fellow sisters never contracted the disease, and they were instrumental in bringing twentieth-century nursing to the sick and dying there. She, too, is one of our newest saints. Many of the remaining patients were able to make the long journey to Rome to witness her canonization in October, 2012.

Back on Oahu, Hedy and I settled into Hawaiian living. We enjoyed the beach community of Kailua because it reminded us of Redondo Beach, where we had grown up. Within a couple of years, my brother, Dan, decided to move back to Maine with his family, so we dissolved our partnership and I took over the Hawaiian agency we had built together. The company had an idea to have an office on each major Hawaiian island. I was content with our Oahu office, and the agents loved going on road trips to the outer islands. But there was no fighting upper management, and within a few months, some of our managers relocated to the outer isles to oversee a small number of agents on the Big Isle, Maui, and Kauai. This meant I was traveling to each of those islands periodically, which wasn't so bad. But things were definitely becoming very spread out for me, as I was soon overseeing our office in Anchorage, Alaska, and making routine trips there.

In due time, Camille entered a pre-school known as the Tiny Tots program. Hedy helped at the preschool co-op, along with the other moms who were the teachers. The moms volunteered to teach one day out of the week. One of the kids' moms was not always able to be there, so in her place would be her close friend, who happened to be an OB/GYN doctor. Everyone called her Doc. Doc would invite Hedy and the kids over to her house to play in her pool and chase her cats around, and she shared with our kids her love of gardening. She was a reputable doctor with a cheerful demeanor, but she also performed abortions when her patients requested not to keep their child.

Somehow, by the grace of God, we obtained our goal of keeping Hedy home as a full-time mom until the kids were ready for school. As Hedy was looking at getting back into nursing on a part-time basis, Doc was happy to hire Hedy to help out at her office. In her friend's absence, Doc would volunteer at the preschool one day a week as well. Hedy became good friends with

Doc in the weeks that followed, both through work as well as at the preschool.

After a few months, Doc told my wife a story. She said that one day, out of the blue, while the kids were on the playground, she watched our daughter Camille gliding back and forth on the swings. A classmate was off to the side watching her, but she was very shy. Camille asked the girl if she wanted to swing. After a silent nod, Camille got off and helped the other girl get on the swing and began pushing her. Doc had watched this innocent interaction, and she was impressed that a child could be so thoughtful and have it come so naturally.

This was at a time in Doc's professional career when she had questioned the morality of abortion and her role in it. It dawned on her that she had been partially responsible for taking away moments such as these from the children she aborted. Her heart was moved by the kindness of Camille. From that day forward, Doc would not perform another abortion. You can't really explain this transformation other than to say that only God could use a child to make such a life-changing impact on another. When Hedy told me this, it gave me "chicken-skin" to think God had used our daughter for such an incredible good. Camille had no idea how profound her gesture was, but in time, she would. We will be forever grateful to Doc for allowing Hedy to work at her office, which gave her the experience to then work at some of the local hospitals. Fifteen years later, Camille would be working at Doc's office during the summer's home from college. Events such as these strengthened my faith in Jesus, and it was awesome to see him working miracles in those around me. However, with work and everything else vying for my attention, this enthusiasm unfortunately became short-lived.

As Camille and Andrew settled into school, despite how busy my work had become, I made it a point to get them active in soccer, and I enjoyed being their coach. Like most kids, they also got into piano lessons, ballet, basketball, volleyball, tennis and even surfing. The music of the Beatles was still very relevant to me, and it was a sad day in 2001 when I learned that George Harrison had died from cancer. If there is one band the kids will remember being played at home or in the car, it is the Beatles. I once took the family to see a performance of a Beatles tribute band that was touring the nation with a stop in Honolulu. That was kind of a dream of mine, too—to be Ringo in a Beatles tribute band. How much fun that would be! I wasn't quite sure I would ever find capable musicians who had the same passion for the Beatles as I did, especially on an island where the popular musical genre was a mix of reggae and Hawaiian known as Jawaiian.

I felt it was my duty as their father to get them familiar with the Beatles catalog and, for fun, to know which Beatle was singing which song. I must admit, they got very good, especially Camille, at being able to remember the "Paul" songs, and which ones Ringo and George were singing. Andrew, on the other hand, took to the drums and was gifted with natural rhythm—ever since he was eight months old, the kid could keep a beat.

It was also about this time that I got word that Ivan, one of the Medjugorje visionaries, would be visiting some churches on Oahu. One of his stops was our parish in Kailua. Hedy, the kids, and I were anxious to see this part of Medjugorje come to Hawaii. Like he had done so many times before, Ivan graciously explained the story of Medjugorje, his village, and the messages he received from the Blessed Mother to give to the world. It brought back those incredible memories of being back in Medjugorje. Camille and Andrew were still a bit too young to understand it all, but they remained well-behaved while he spoke.

Our family with Medjugorje visionary, Ivan, after his talk at St. Anthony's Church, Kailua, Oahu.

Though I was excited to see Ivan again and hear what he had to say, there was nothing new under the sun for me, and I was at a time in my life when I was simply focused on my career and trying to be the best dad I could be to my children. Admittedly, my spiritual growth was in a slump.

We attended Mass on Sundays, but beyond that, I didn't have or make much time for my spiritual life. I had joined the Knights of Columbus and Hedy and I became involved with Marriage Encounter, but I was rarely reading anything spiritual, nor praying the rosary, and I would rarely crack the Bible. I had read so much in prior years, and I was a bit burned out. I was focused on my management career instead. I received numerous awards and became one of the leading regional managers in the company. However, in time, my style of management began to conflict with upper management. No matter the success, it was never quite good enough for the powers that were. Politics, power plays, and favoritism became the rule of the day and overshadowed the business I had established. The higher I climbed up the corporate ladder, the worse the view became.

It wasn't all drama, however. I did make time for Hedy and the kids. We enjoyed hikes and days at the beach, but it seemed like time was always becoming harder and harder to come by. My priorities seemed to shift, and it happened so unconsciously. It has been said that to stand still in your faith is to go backward. That was the case with me. In time, I would make the difficult decision to take a huge pay cut and wean myself from management, simplifying my career by becoming a salesperson once again without the stress and responsibility of overseeing two states. I would never regret it.

Once out of management, my stress level felt like it reduced by half. Through my parish, I had met a lady named Pam Aqui. Pam and her husband Mike belonged to the Benedictine Monastery as oblates. An oblate is someone who joins an order as a lay or married person and is involved in its ministry and prayer life. Pam would often talk of her trips up to the monastery located in the hills above Waialua on the North Shore of Oahu. She would often go on and on about how beautiful it was up there, and she talked about each of the priests, sisters, and brothers who lived in the community. There were Sister Mary Jo McEnany and Father Michael Sawyer, who were spiritual directors for retreats held at a retreat center in Kalihi Valley six to eight times per year. Pam always seemed to have stories about them or about other people whose lives had been transformed by these retreats. What intrigued me was that Pam herself was a convert and had visited Medjugorje some years earlier with Sister Mary Jo and Father Michael.

It was coming back to me now. I recalled how a few years earlier, while attending a morning weekday Mass, a lady named Auntie Millie stopped me in the parking lot before going to my car. She handed me a brochure and told me it contained information about an upcoming spiritual retreat by the BCC or Basic Christian Community. She said it was a great opportunity to connect with God. It sounded nice, and I was very much into retreats, but to break away for an entire weekend then was just too difficult. I thanked her for the information and told her I would think about it. I never did think about it much beyond that; that is, until Pam brought it freshly into my mind once again.

With more time on my hands, Hedy and I opened up a retail store, and Pam was one of our first hires. We thought it would be a fun venture. The fun turned into yet another huge commitment of time, but this was our baby and there was no upper management to contend with, so we were fine with it.

Pam talked about this Basic Christian Community retreat like it was a life-changing experience. I thought change was possible for some, but I had already been to Medjugorje and had my life-changing experience. I didn't think I had much more to gain. I had become so involved with everything around me. I had lost touch with my faith, but my pride told me otherwise. I knew this, but I didn't want to admit it. I decided to go and told Pam I was in for the next retreat. Hedy would be able to spend that weekend with the kids, and Pam was gracious enough to manage the store during the entire weekend in my absence.

Chapter 8

ALL YOU NEED IS LOVE

"Dear children! I wish to thank you for all the sacrifices and I invite you to the greatest sacrifice, the sacrifice of love. Without love, you are not able to accept either me or my Son. Without love, you cannot give an account of your experiences to others. Therefore, dear children, I call you to begin to live love within yourselves. Thank you for having responded to my call."

Medjugorje Message, March 27, 1986

It was all set for the fall of 2004. I would finally make the Basic Christian Community retreat. I went, and sure enough, it was life-changing. Pam had told me ahead of time that God was there, and that I would see God. Sure enough, I did see God. I cannot really offer any explanation of what is experienced at a BCC retreat. It just is. I saw God in the beauty of the grounds of the retreat center, but more importantly in the eyes and faces of those working and serving on the retreat, along with the other participants. I had attended numerous retreats before, but this one left a lasting fire. There was an immediate acceptance of each other regardless of who they were, what they looked like, and where they came from. The people were full of unconditional love, and they went out of their way to make sure each participant was as comfortable as could be, and there was simply an aura of holiness that seemed to emanate from the grounds. The essence of it was love—love of God and love of neighbor. I was reminded that this is what matters and what life is about.

As spiritual leaders for the retreat, Father Michael and Sister Mary Jo provided just enough catechism blended with the messages of the Gospel to help support the many stories of conversion narrated by several lay people throughout the weekend. The many volunteers who were there to serve us did so with love in their hearts, which was very touching. The retreat was an emotional rollercoaster, bringing about intense moments of joy, fun, laughter, and somberness throughout the weekend. I felt the same power of the Holy Spirit as I did in Medjugorje. What was exciting was that now that I had attended this retreat, I was welcome to help out on future retreats. Furthermore, there were weekly cell groups that met all over the island. "Cell" meant that each of us were cells interconnected within one body—the body of Christ. Those who had attended past retreats and wanted to continue that sense of community in studying the Bible and sharing faith stories with close friends in an intimate setting were always welcome.

Ah, community! Community is what I had been yearning for all this time. I had felt a strong sense of community with the staff of Veritas some fourteen years earlier, but since we had moved around the country, I didn't feel much community, even with my own parish church. Pam and her husband Mike had an active cell group they facilitated, and we met (and still meet) every Wednesday at their home.

I had finally found a Catholic community that helped invigorate my faith in the same way Medjugorje did. As in Medjugorje, I discovered that the love you receive at these retreats is genuine love. Those who work on the retreats have servants' hearts and gain as much from serving as the participants do receiving. Like the residents of Medjugorje, those who serve in BCC give wholly of themselves before, during, and after any retreat.

With the BCC community, I hold myself accountable more often, and I'm reminded to live my life as Christ would through the intimacy of my cell group. Through the BCC cell group, an intimate connection is made with fellow Christians—they accept and support me, as well as pray for me, and we become an extended family. This is the critical link that I feel is missing in our parishes as a whole. Sometimes, a parish is just too large to express one's intimate needs, questions, and concerns.

I often fall short in my spiritual life. Now I have a deeper awareness of my need for community. I'm not a theologian, but with all the spiritual reading I've done, I do know better. To live one's faith is a decision. Once you decide for God, then you have yourself and everyone around looking at you and holding you accountable. That decision is crystal clear, but it is not always easy to follow through as God desires. I do take time to pray each day in some way and involve God in the decisions I make. I'm reminded of the importance of being involved in some kind of spiritual community.

After transitioning out of management, and then Hedy's and my short-lived retail store, I thought about a new career involving real estate. Within a year, I earned my license and went to work with one of the big firms on Oahu. I cherished the extra time with the kids and the balance that was restored to my schedule. As I got established in my new career, I hung up my life insurance license and worked to become a real estate broker, while still dabbling in property and casualty insurance for the homeowners I represent.

Mom and Dad had always been good about visiting us in Hawaii each year, but Dad had been battling cancer off and on for several years. My brothers, sister, and I successfully planned their fiftieth wedding anniversary in the summer of 2006 in California. It was a special day when friends, cousins, aunts, and uncles I hadn't seen in years had crossed the country to be with us. Old friends from Saint Lawrence were there, and it was like stepping back in time.

Also on hand to renew Mom and Dad's vows was Doug Ferraro, formerly Father Doug Ferraro. After becoming a monsignor and working at the cathedral downtown, he had decided to leave the priesthood around the time we were in Seattle. They were priming him for big positions when all he wanted was to be a parish priest. I remember sending him a letter letting him know that, though I was sad to see him leave his ministry, I wished him well in his new life and let him know what a positive impact he had on me when I was a kid. It was so nice to see him again after so many years.

Dad had just completed some rounds of chemo, and things were looking up. He had beaten prostate cancer and bladder cancer before, and kept the disease at bay even though it had got into his lymph nodes. Then in May 2007 we received the news that the cancer had entered his pancreas. I knew that wasn't good. Few people live more than a year once it reaches that organ, and the doctors had given dad about seven months. We all agreed to meet in Florida with our kids to have another reunion, which we realized might be the last time Dad saw us all together. We celebrated that time together as a family, and it was great. A few weeks later back in Hawaii, I was depressed thinking about Dad and feeling guilty for being so far away. Dad had been a lifetime Chicago Cubs fan. After he retired, he worked as an usher at Wrigley Field for nostalgia's sake when he and Mom bought a condo on Lakeshore Drive to spend the summers there a few years after we had moved to Hawaii.

I decided to see if the Cubs could bring him some cheer. I sent them a letter telling them that Dad was now dying, and that he had been an usher there several years back, and there were few days that Dad wouldn't be watching the Cubs when they were playing on TV. I simply asked them if there was anything they could send him to brighten his day—an autographed baseball, a signed picture from one of the players, anything really—and that it would be very much appreciated.

I didn't tell Mom or anyone about this, since I didn't know if they would even respond. Mom called me a couple of weeks after. She said there was a letter sent from the Cubs on their official letterhead to Dad. They said that they were grateful for his years of appreciation for the team, and they were rooting him on in his fight with cancer, and they wished him the best. With that letter was an 8x10 picture taken of the famous Wrigley Field marquee. The marquee was lit up with the words, "CUBS SIGN CARL MUTH." Mom said that in fifty-one years of marriage, she had never seen Dad cry before—nor had any of us. When he received that, he wept. With my parents having grown up in Chicago, I always knew Dad was a Cubs fan, but I never before knew just how much. When Mom put Dad on the phone, I could tell he was choked up about it. He said it was the best gift he had ever received. He asked me what he could do to thank me. I said, "Dad, I didn't do much. This is coming from your team that you have stood by all these years. You don't have to thank me."

"I know," he said, "but there must be something I can do."

I said, "Dad, you write them back and thank them for the letter and the picture, and you let them know how much it meant to you. That's all you need to do." A few days later when I called him, he was proud to tell me that a thank-you card had been sent to Wrigley Field.

In early October, Hedy, the kids, and I flew out to Florida to be with Mom and Dad. It was a strange trip to plan and look forward to, as we knew this would be the last time we'd see my father. Dad had a rough several weeks just before we had arrived, but now with this latest batch of chemo, he seemed to be doing better—at least with regard to his energy levels. We went out to eat a couple of times, played games, went to a movie, and walked along the pier near their home in Saint Petersburg. Dad would get tired, but even he was surprised that he felt well enough to do all the things we did that week. We also watched on TV what would be the last Cubs games of that year. A winning season brought them to the brink of the playoffs, but they ultimately lost to the Arizona Diamondbacks in a 3-0 shutout. After the last game, Dad looked at me and, with a twinkle in his eye, said, "There's always next season." Of course, that's what all Cubs fans say to one another, but I could tell in his voice that he was being optimistically sarcastic. He knew he wouldn't be on this Earth next season. It was just Dad and I in the room. I asked him, "Dad, you gonna be okay?"

He said, "Dennis, I'll be fine. I think of all the people who haven't been able to live the life I have. Married to your mother for fifty years, traveling the world as we have, and being healthy enough to do it all—we've been very fortunate. We're happy the way all you kids ended up...we've been very blessed and we've had great friends along the way. I've been very blessed. I'm ready to go."

Our last family photo with Mom and Dad.

With that amount of courage, I knew Dad was accepting of his fate. The uncertainty of how and when each of us will die can be a bit scary, and Dad no doubt felt some of that. I know Dad was a believer and looked forward to soon being with Jesus. Camille and Andrew got to spend those last days with their grandfather, and it was always a bit uncomfortable when we were together because we knew this would be our last time with Dad and Grandpa, but we carried on like there would be a next time.

I can't recall why, but for some reason Hedy and the kids left on an earlier flight home that day than me. So I drove myself to the airport with Mom and Dad both in the car. After the thirty-minute drive to Tampa, I pulled up to the terminal, got out, grabbed my suitcase, and set it on the curb and absolutely dreaded what was about to happen. I looked at Mom and gave her a kiss and a big hug. As I went to embrace Dad standing next to her, I could see the tears in his eyes. As the tears welled up in me, I whispered, "Dad...I'm gonna see you again, we'll be together...I love you so much."

Dad replied in a soft-spoken voice, "I love you too, Dennis."

We gave each other a big, long hug. As our bodies separated, he did something he had never done to me before. He grabbed my face in his hands and he kissed me on my cheek as if all his love was being radiated through his lips. Dad had never been that touchy-feely. This was the warmest thing I had ever felt from him. I hated to go and wanted to stay with them. I couldn't. I couldn't just see us three standing there sobbing, either. Dad wouldn't take his eyes off me, and as I was grabbing my suitcase from the curb I looked at him and I said, "I'm gonna see you again, Dad."

With watery eyes he said, "You will. We'll see you again—and it's okay. I love you, Dennis."

Walking backward toward the glass terminal doors, I waved to them. As I got inside the terminal, I turned away from my parents. I went to the nearest bathroom and, once inside, I found a stall, locked the door, and for the next ten minutes I cried like a baby.

It wasn't long after that visit that Dad's health went downhill. Hospice was a huge support for both him and Mom. As Dad became weaker, they brought in a hospital bed and set it up next to the bed in their room. Mom said that Dad didn't like sleeping apart from her and would often leave the hospital bed and crawl over into her bed to be next to her. With my oldest brother, Dave, and his family close by, they also became an excellent support system for Mom and Dad.

I'd call regularly and speak with Dad when he had energy and would have him speak to Hedy, Camille, and Andrew if he was up to it. He stopped eating after a while, and though most patients with pancreatic cancer have a very painful experience as death approaches, Dad was free of pain up until the day he died. Mom was always happy to report that though he was becoming skin and bones, he was comfortable and not in much, if any, pain. That to me was an answered prayer. God would take him peacefully.

The last time I spoke with my Dad, I had just pulled into a parking garage. It was a Friday. Mom had said the doctor thought he might not make it through the weekend. He was coherent, but I could tell it was hard for him to speak because he was so weak and each breath seemed to be such an effort for him. I could tell he wanted to speak, and he told me he was okay and not to worry about anything. He was ready to go and was at peace. This was really good-bye now. We spoke for another minute or two before he was too tired to say anymore, and I just told him that we were all praying for him and we all loved him so much. He would soon see his mother, father, and sister who had passed away years before. In time, we would see him again too.

The next evening, December 16, 2007, I was in my car driving home from a band rehearsal. That whole day was very strange. It was as if I was in denial and everything was going to be okay with

Dad—that he was going to be fine. I tried to think that this was not Dad's last day, and that he would hang in there. There would be more phone calls, more conversations, more "I love you's." But I was kidding myself. As I was driving, my cell phone rang. The caller ID showed it was my sister, Julie, in California. I pulled the car over into a parking lot. I just knew.

All Things Must Pass

Julie said my name in a sobbing voice. It was hard for her to speak it, but I knew what it was. She had just got off the phone with Mom. Dad had just died. Time seemed to stop, and the reality of his death felt like a truck-load of bricks falling on my chest. I asked Julie to pray with me, and so we did. Driving home in a numbed state, I kept it together until I got inside the house. As she sat on the couch, Hedy could see it in my eyes. Without saying a word to her, I collapsed on her lap and cried my deepest cry.

My brothers, sister, and I all were there with mom for Dad's service in Florida. Many old friends and relatives were on hand to pay their final respects. Mom asked if I wanted to present a eulogy to Dad, along with a couple of other friends and his cousin. There was so much to say about Dad—how does one condense such emotion and love? I wanted to sum up Dad's life and the positive effect he had on so many people, but I wasn't sure what to write. Somehow, the words just came out...

Eulogy For a Father

Dad taught us each to be a person of substance—to be devoted to the things you love most. There are few things that could surpass the devotion Dad had for the Cubs. It must be a Chicago thing. Loving a team that is notorious for losing is not very admirable. Yet the lesson here is the hope that Dad, and any Cubs fan, has: That one can and should believe in miracles, to dream and dream big, and that the best is yet to come. I know from where Dad stands today, he is saying that to us all—that the best is yet to come. Dad taught us to apply another important message as a Cubs fan. You may not always like the Cubs, and they will be sure to disappoint, but you love them anyway. Just as you may not always like a certain person in your life, as they too will disappoint, you should love them anyway.

The only thing that surpassed Dad's undying devotion to the Cubs would be his devotion to his lifelong friend and spouse of fifty-one years, our mom, Lori. Mom always was, and will always be, the love of his life. The love they shared was truly heaven-sent. Ever faithful, he treated Mom as a queen. Their love was without fail and unwavering.

Mom and Dad were truly a couple. They loved doing things together. In fact, I can hardly think of an activity the other one was engaged in that did not include the other. Playing cards, golfing, reading, traveling, watching sports, going to a concert, being with friends, going to church, spending time with the grandkids—these were always done as a couple. For fifty-one years, they were as inseparable as a couple on their honeymoon. There was a certain something in the marriage of Mom and Dad. It was a love that surpasses understanding, and is something that anyone who has been around them noticed. People always commented on how in love they were and what a great couple they'd been. I could never put a finger on it other than to say that they were truly meant for each other. Their marriage was an inspiration to all of us.

Lastly, today needs to be a joyous day. Dad would not like us to be sad. He's seen enough sad days as a Cubs fan. We need to celebrate dad's new life. Dad belongs in heaven, and he is going to help us all get there. He is anxiously waiting to greet us when it is our turn to go.

Mom, few of us can realize the loss that you suffer. I know Dad would want you to continue to live your life to the fullest as you always have. You are not alone. If you look around this church, you will see that these are the people who will continue to travel with you, play cards with you, golf with you, pray with you, share stories with you and most of all, love you. Know that each of us will be here for you.

In closing, I think that as kids we've turned out okay. I know Dad is proud of us. The same traits that made Dad a great man will hopefully continue on in us, and his grandchildren for generations to come. There are granddaughters who will grow into women and grandsons who will become men and carry on the Muth name. A name that will continue to be mispronounced by many, yet will have meaning far beyond the courage which defines it. A name that will invoke the memory of a man we know as Carl, but a man they know as Grandpa. A loving man who will leave a positive imprint on all of his children and grandchildren, forever.

"I'm prepared for death because I don't believe in it. I think it's just getting out of one car and getting into another."
John Lennon, 1969

Chapter 9

I CALL YOUR NAME

Two weeks before Dad died in 2007, I was asked to give a talk about my conversion experience to the participants at a BCC retreat. Since I have always felt that the Beatles played a part in my being led to Medjugorje, I dedicated my talk to John, Paul, George, and Ringo. This introduced me to the music director for that retreat, whose name was Nolet. He was also a huge Beatles fan. More than just a music director, Nolet was a fantastic musician and singer.

That evening, he strummed for me on his acoustic guitar some of his favorite Beatles songs, and he sang and played them with incredible accuracy. Like anyone else who has ever heard Nolet perform, I was speechless. I discovered that he was not only involved in serving at the BCC retreats, but he and his wife were active in their parish as choir directors and Confirmation directors. Nolet had long been an accomplished musician, very talented with bass, guitar, and singing. However, he had not been doing much more with music outside of church.

It wasn't too long before he approached me with the idea of forming a Beatles tribute band on Oahu. I had been waiting for such an invite for twenty years! He would be Paul, and, acting naturally, I would be Ringo. Now we had to find John and George. A band that I was playing in had recently broken up, but I thought one of the guitarists from that band would be a good fit. Alastar was a great guitarist, and he did look slightly like George. I knew he could pick up the parts. He was in. Now if we could just find a "John."

Nolet recalled an old musician friend of his on the island, whom he had grown up with in the Philippines. This friend also loved the Beatles, and Nolet thought he could be our "John." Nolet was able to contact his friend Sonny, only to find out that he hadn't played guitar or sung in more than ten years. Bummer. Nolet decided to meet with him anyhow and just have a casual jam—just the two of them—to see what would happen. They played song after song of the Beatles, and it was as if they had been playing together for years. The chemistry was perfect, and so now it was time for the four of us to get together to see if we clicked. When we did, the result was fantastic. There were some obvious rough edges to work out, but within a few short months, we would be ready for our first gig. After a couple of name changes, we finalized our band's name as "Day in the Life" after the brilliant song that appeared on the *Sgt. Peppers* album. Things were getting better all the time.

Conversion - Let It Be

"Dear children! Also today, with great joy in my heart, I call you to conversion. Little children, do not forget that you are all important in this great plan, which God leads through Medjugorje. God desires to convert the entire world and to call it to salvation and to the way towards Himself, who is the beginning and the end of every being. In a special way, little children, from the depth of my heart, I call you all to open yourselves to this great grace that God gives you through my presence here. I desire to thank each of you for the sacrifices and prayers. I am with you and I bless you all. Thank you for having responded to my call."

Medjugorje Message, June 25, 2007

So in retrospect, the Beatles led me to Medjugorje, and through Nolet, BCC led me to my dream of playing in a Beatles tribute band. It is surprising that after more than thirty years, there are people who still do not know about Medjugorje. That was one of the reasons I felt compelled to write this book.

I've discovered when you abandon yourself, you feel liberated in making yourself available to the Lord and what he can do for you. It is a constant inner struggle to want to fill the needs of self and serve others. You cannot really do both simultaneously—it is a matter of which one you choose to submit to.

Do I long to go back to Medjugorje someday? Absolutely. Do I need to go back there? No, but I certainly wouldn't mind either. I must admit early on that I was somewhat of an addict to Medjugorje. I wanted to know everything I could about what was happening there and receive the latest messages. But that soon gave way to my learning phase, and in the end, I know that was the purpose of my trip to Medjugorje. It was to rediscover my Catholic faith and learn more about it. I was coming home. All that learning has served me well, but in the end, I am reminded that it is about peace and love. We are called to be peaceful and to love God and others. How can we love another if we are not at peace with ourselves? Peace is a prerequisite for love.

After I fell in love with Jesus, his mother, Mary, and the Holy Spirit, I fell in love with Hedy and my two children who followed. As I pursued my career and moved around the country, I lost my way a little bit. I wasn't sinning any more than I normally would, but I just wasn't doing much to enhance my faith life, either. Basic Christian Community allowed me to become one with an active community of like-minded Christian Catholics. This rejuvenated my faith in a huge way and returned to me the "fire" of the Spirit that I had received so many years earlier in Medjugorje.

I've learned that conversion is not something that has to be limited to a single occasion. It can, and should, happen to us throughout our lives. I was content after Medjugorje. I felt the Spirit would remain with me forever. I was wrong. I became distracted, busy, and over time my faith life suffered. I didn't make time for God. Of course, as a husband and father, that is my primary ministry, and only my wife and kids can judge me on how I have fared there. I'd like to think so far, so good—but there's always room for improvement.

Hedy and I in recent years.

Mary, our Blessed Mother, is stressing conversion over and over again in her messages. The more we convert, the greater our impact will be with the world through others we meet. *Convert*, in the sense of the messages of Medjugorje, is an action verb. That means we must do something on our end for it to transpire.

Saint Paul, in his letter to the Ephesians states, "You must no longer live as the Gentiles do, in the futility of their minds; that is not how you learned Christ, assuming that you have heard of him and were taught in him, as truth is in Jesus, that you should put away the old self of your former way of life, corrupted through deceitful desires, and be renewed in the spirit of your minds, and put on the new self, created in God's way in righteous and holiness of truth."

Throughout history, great and holy men and women have come along to remind the faithful of what being a Christian is about. It is not about pomp and riches or power or authority. As Saint Francis, Saint Damien, Mother Teresa, and our newest pope have shown us, it is about love and service to others. By their actions, they have exemplified this much more than their words ever could. In the Bible, John 15 says, "I am the vine, you are the branches. Whoever remains in me and I in him will bear much fruit, because without me you can do nothing...If you remain in me and my words remain in you, ask for whatever you want, and it will be done for you. By this is my Father glorified, that you bear much fruit and become my disciples. As the Father loves me, so I also love you. Remain in my love."

Perhaps my journey to and from Medjugorje was really a microcosm of my greater journey in Christ. Haven't there always been people who are put in our lives for no reason other than to give us some inspiration and/or direction? Perhaps they are angels. Is it any coincidence that of all the other billions of people we could "bump into," that we happen to bump into these "guides" at a certain moment in time?

From the Beatles tour driver who first brought the Cathedral to our attention, to our meeting with Father John in Liverpool, and then to the lady in the bookstore showing me where Medjugorje was—they were all part of God's plan in my life. The train ride getting there could be classified as my "desert" experience. It was as if I needed to be purged of the comforts that I knew so well to prepare myself for the messages I would soon hear in Medjugorje. I needed to be hot, sweaty, surrounded by toxic cigarette smoke, hungry, and parched with thirst to remind myself that the road to Christian living will not always be comfortable and smooth, nor what I'm used to.

Yet, as the suffering of Good Friday prepares us for the glory of the Resurrection, that lonely, unbearable train ride gave way to greener pastures and an abundance of food and hospitality, thanks to my angelic guides like Mrs. Vrbanec and Vera, the travel agent. I know now it was no coincidence. Unbeknownst to them, God placed them in my midst to guide and serve me. Through them and others along the way, my journey to Medjugorje was realized and made complete.

It is extraordinary to ponder God's signs through the people who come into our lives and shape who we become. It amazes me how some of these people are fleeting and are out of our lives as quickly as they entered. Yet their influence remains with us. It could have been a phrase or even a word they said that causes us to see things in a new light. Yet how much more extraordinary is it to ponder how we, ourselves, are being used in this way for those around us. Even without knowing it, we could make a difference in the life of another, as a little girl on a swing did for a doctor. If God so wills it, it will be done.

In looking back on my European travels that summer and especially to that holy place called Medjugorje, it wasn't so much of a spiritual journey to God as much as it was a journey to myself and to my soul. Mary, Jesus, and God were with me long before I left California. I didn't need to go to Medjugorje to find them, and yet I did. How long it would have taken for me to truly discover their existence in my heart will forever be a mystery. For this reason, it was important that I traveled where I did, when I did, and how I did, as this process—this journey—made me discover them when I most needed to.

We are all seeking truth. We wonder what the bigger picture is in all of this, and we long to be in tune with our spiritual nature. We want answers. We want solutions. I believe some of the answers lie in these moments of conversion. Through conversion, we may find what we are looking for. The Blessed Mother is asking us to convert our hearts to God. She knows that only then can we find true peace. We are all spiritual beings. But, secular living gets in the way, and we become distracted. It also takes effort on our part, which causes us to leave our comfort zones. It's extraordinary to see those who have converted their lives and end up in service to others and finally find their purpose. Only in giving are they able to receive.

Ephesians 1:17 says, "May the God of our Lord Jesus Christ, the Father of glory, give you a Spirit of wisdom and revelation resulting in knowledge of him. May the eyes of your hearts be enlightened, that you may know what is the hope that belongs to his call." My own conversion could be summed up in this verse.

Through the Blessed Mother, God gave me a spirit of wisdom and revelation, which gave me a greater awareness of his glory. The eyes of my heart, indeed, were enlightened on that mountain in Bosnia-Herzegovina named Mount Krizevac, and I was called to live the messages that subsequently came to me. I pray they that they may also move you in a similar way.

EPILOGUE

As I listened to Ivan give his presentation that evening in Hawaii Kai, he spoke so simply on what we as Christians need to do: less self, more service. Ivan has been called to minister to the youth and be an example of living the messages of Medjugorje. Never before had I heard him or any other visionary go into such detail about those initial days of Mary's appearances. The fear, wonder, and excitement he experienced were an astounding first-hand account. He went on to explain how his life was completely transformed as a result.

The messages he imparted were not contrary to the Gospel, and actually conveyed the same level of urgency that we find in the Bible. The messages given to him by the Blessed Mother were meant to be stern at times, and comforting at others—like we would expect coming from a mother. He reiterated the need for peace, conversion, prayer, and fasting, and that if we have peace in our hearts, we won't be filled with anxiety or worry.

As the kids and I drove home that evening, my mind began drifting back to when I was in Medjugorje. The simple life of the villagers, who were farming, and tending to their vineyards, and taking care of the pilgrims. The crowds gathered both on Mount Krizevac and Apparition Hill on Mount Podbrdo. People praying together at every turn, and hearing the sounds of roosters crowing. This certainly seemed idyllic, but this was reality. Such a place does exist. Some may even say it's heaven on Earth. Maybe I do want to go back, and perhaps some day I will.

For now, Medjugorje is a place inside my heart that I pray will never leave me. It's a place where peace and love combine with God's grace—teaching me, comforting me, preparing me, calling me by name again and again into the stillness of my soul, into the grandeur of the universe which is him. I am listening, and I am here.

"I, a prisoner for the Lord, urge you to live in a manner worthy of the call you have received, with all humility and gentleness, with patience, bearing with one another through love, striving to preserve the unity of the spirit through the bond of peace: one body and one Spirit, as you were also called to the one hope of your call, one Lord, one faith, one baptism, one God and Father of all, who is over all and through all and all in all." (Ephesians 4:1)

"And in the end, the love you take is equal to the love you make."
—Paul McCartney

APPENDIX

Do You Want To Know A Secret?

Our Lady has confided secrets to the six visionaries. These secrets relate to each of the children, the Parish of Saint James, as well as the world. Mary has said that when all six children have the ten secrets, she will stop appearing to them on a daily basis. As of this writing, Mirjana, Ivanka and Jakov have received all ten secrets and no longer experience daily apparitions.

Mirjana Dragicevic has an apparition once a year on her birthday (March 18), and since 1987, she has received an apparition on the second of each month to pray for all unbelievers. She is married and has two daughters and resides in Medjugorje.

Ivanka Ivankovic, whose primary intention is to pray for families, stopped having daily apparitions on May 7, 1985, when she received her tenth secret. The Blessed Mother has promised to appear to Ivanka on the anniversary of the first apparition, June 25, and has kept to that ever since. Ivanka is married with three children and also lives in Medjugorje.

Jakov Colo, the youngest of the seers who was only ten years old when the apparitions began, has been told by the Blessed Mother to pray for the sick. His last daily apparition was September 12, 1998, when he received the tenth secret. The Blessed Mother still appears to Jakov on Christmas Day each year. He is married with three children and still resides in Medjugorje.

Vicka Ivankovic was also asked by Our Lady to pray for the sick. She has received nine secrets and still has daily apparitions. In 1986, she suffered high fevers, severe headaches, and comas from an inoperable brain tumor. In February 1988, she wrote three sealed letters: one to her confessor, one to the priests residing in Medjugorje, and lastly, to the Bishop's Commission investigating the apparitions at the time. They were told not to open the letter until she instructed them to do so. Seven months later, she asked them each to open the letters in the presence of two witnesses. The letter stated that her tumor and suffering was a gift from God, and its purpose was to heal the illnesses of sinners, and that she would now be cured of the tumor. After a series of medical tests, her tumor was confirmed as completely gone. She is now married with two children and lives near Medjugorje.

Ivan Dragicevic also has received nine secrets and receives daily apparitions. He has been asked by the Blessed Mother to especially pray for priests and youth throughout the world. He married an American girl, and they have four children. They reside half of the year in her hometown of Boston and the rest of the year in Medjugorje. Ivan regularly travels around the world spreading the messages of Our Lady to various churches and conferences. Regardless of where he is, he continues to have a daily apparition at 6:40 p.m. local time.

Marija Pavlovic, having received nine secrets, also sees the Blessed Mother each day. She receives the Blessed Mother's monthly message on the twenty-fifth of each month for the world. She especially prays for all the souls in purgatory. Marija is married with four children and lives most of the year in Italy. She visits Medjugorje throughout the year.

When the remaining three visionaries receive their last secret, there will be a series of warnings for the world, which will occur in Mirjana's lifetime. There will be a period of grace and conversion between the first and second warning. The third secret will be a permanent, visible supernatural and indestructible sign on Apparition Hill where the Blessed Mother first appeared. She will urge conversion and reconciliation at this time. It is said this permanent sign will lead many to God and convert their lives and provide healing for others.

The secrets are of a serious nature, and though some effects can be lessened through prayer and fasting, others will not. These chastisements will take place for the sins of the world. In her messages, Mary has said, "You have forgotten that with prayer and fasting you can ward off wars, suspend natural laws."

This is why she continues to appear. There is an urgency in her tone, and she reminds us that right now, as you read this, we are in a valuable state of grace. Now is the time to convert our hearts back to God. In an interview in October 1985, the visionary Mirjana said, "There never was an age such as this one; never before was God honored and respected less than now, never before have so few prayed to him. Everything seems to be more important than God. This is the reason she cries so much."

In March 2010, the Holy See announced that the Congregation for the Doctrine of Faith was forming an investigative commission, composed of bishops, theologians, and other experts, under the leadership of Cardinal Camillo Ruini, who was once the Vicar General for the Diocese of Rome. The commission is expected to report any findings to the congregation, which has responsibility for any possible judgment on the case, but will not report any final word until the apparitions cease. As of this writing, the church is still reserving judgment as the apparitions continue.

"Dear children! I desire to place all of you under my mantle and protect you from all satanic attacks. Today is a day of peace, but in the whole world there is a great lack of peace. That is why I call you all to build a new world of peace with me through prayer. This I cannot do without you, and this is why I call all of you with my motherly love and God will do the rest. So, open yourselves to God's plan and to his designs to be able to cooperate with him for peace and for everything that is good. Do not forget that your life does not belong to you, but is a gift with which you must bring joy to others and lead them to eternal life. May the tenderness of the little Jesus always accompany you. Thank you for having responded to my call."

Medjugorje Message, December 25, 1992

ACKNOWLEDGEMENTS

I'd like to thank God for all of his greatness and blessings. For Jesus' redemptive and unfailing love that he has for everyone one of us, and his Mother, Mary, for her comfort and relentless calling to us, her children.

This book would not be possible if it were not for the inspiration and support of many friends and family. In particular, my parents, Carl and Lori Muth, sister Julie, brothers Dave and Dan, Tom Maxwell, who taught me much more about life than playing drums, and Matt Jones, for reminding me to live in the moment.

To those who were instrumental in providing me valuable feedback and counsel with the writing of this book: Pam and Mike Aqui, Dave and Mary Bird, Darlene Dela Cruz, Larry Carstens, Nancy Downes, Tom Ehart, Mike Filce, Raul Perez, Sister Mary Jo McEnany, Nolet Quiason, Dave and Julie Sanders, and my daughter, Camille Muth. Always grateful to the entire BCC ohana, and to "good, good" LeRoy Brown, the angel who reminded me to never put God to the test.

To John, Paul, George, and Ringo, for filling the world with your music, which continues to stand the test of time and unite those of every faith and nationality across the universe.

Lastly, to my wife Hedy, daughter Camille, and son Andrew, who put up with me despite my corniness, child-like humor, and numerous imperfections. You inspire me, and I'm grateful for your love.

To order additional copies of this book go to www.mothermarycomestome.net

To contact the author:

MotherMaryComes@gmail.com

Facebook: Mother Mary Comes To Me. Words of Wisdom From Medjugorje

To order beautiful, one-of-a-kind heirloom rosaries from my friend, Pam: www.heirloomrosaries.com

Made in the USA
Lexington, KY
01 May 2016